THE NEXT LIBRARY LEADERSHIP

THE NEXT LIBRARY LEADERSHIP

Attributes of Academic and Public Library Directors

PETER HERNON, RONALD R. POWELL,
AND ARTHUR P. YOUNG

A Member of the Greenwood Publishing Group

Westport, Connecticut • London

Library of Congress Cataloging-in-Publication Data

Hernon, Peter.
    The next library leadership : attributes of academic and public library directors /
Peter Hernon, Ronald R. Powell, and Arthur P. Young.
        p. cm.
    Includes bibliographical references.
    ISBN 1–56308–992–0 (alk. paper)
    1. Library directors—United States. 2. Academic library directors—United States.
3. Academic libraries—United States—Administration. 4. Public libraries—United
States—Administration. 5. Leadership. I. Powell, Ronald R. II. Young, Arthur P.
III. Title.
Z682.4.A34H47   2003
025.19′7′092—dc21   2003053874

British Library Cataloguing in Publication Data is available.

Library of Congress Catalog Card Number: 2003053874
ISBN: 1–56308–992–0

First published in 2003

Libraries Unlimited, 88 Post Road West, Westport, CT 06881
A Member of the Greenwood Publishing Group, Inc.
www.lu.com

Printed in the United States of America

The paper used in this book complies with the
Permanent Paper Standard issued by the National
Information Standards Organization (Z39.48–1984).

10 9 8 7 6 5 4 3 2 1

Copyright Acknowledgments

The author and publisher gratefully acknowledge the following sources for granting
permission to use their materials:
    Excerpts from *The Headhunter's Edge* by Jeffrey E. Christian, copyright © 2002
by Jeffrey E. Christian. Used by permission of Random House, Inc.
    Excerpts from *Headhunters: Matchmaking in the Labor Market* by William Finlay
and James E. Coverdill. New York: Cornell University Press, 2002, used with permission of the publisher, Cornell University Press.
    Excerpts from Darlene E. Weingand and Noel Ryan, "Managerial Competences
and Skills: A Joint Study in the United States and Canada," *Journal of Library
Administration* 6 (Spring 1985): 23–44.
    Excerpts from James F. Williams II, "Leadership Evaluation and Assessment,"
Journal of Library Administration 32 (3/4) (2001): 145–167; reprinted with
permission.
    Center for Creative Leadership is the author of the material, "360 By Design
Competencies," discussed in Chapter 7. The material discussed was derived from
http://www.ccl.org/products/360bd/competencies.htm. Used by permission of
publisher.

CONTENTS

ILLUSTRATIONS

Tables

Figures

PREFACE

There is a shortage of individuals attracted to professional careers in librarianship. As a result, government agencies, professional associations, libraries, and schools of library and information studies (LIS) are developing strategies to attract people into the profession. During the interviews that we conducted for this book, a number of library directors expressed concern that a continued shortage might ultimately result in a crisis—that is, if the pool of new librarians does not contain individuals who could become the next generation of talented and dynamic directors and leaders in the profession. This book identifies those traits needed by the next generation of academic and public library directors, and it suggests strategies that individuals can use to prepare themselves for leadership positions and the challenges ahead. The book also argues that we all have a stake in the outcome and should invest in those individuals likely to guide the nation's academic and public libraries in the future.

Writing in the late 1960s, Perry D. Morrison conducted "a study of the social origins, educational attainments, vocational experience, and personality characteristics of a group of American academic librarians." Among his findings that pertain to this book are the following traits: "variety of experience is a . . . prominent feature of the careers of chief academic librarians"; the "opportunity to move to another more enriching experience"; a willingness to take advantage of that opportunity; holding the necessary academic and professional education; and possession of relevant "personal qualities and characteristics." In presenting those "personal qualities and characteristics," he described academic librarians as "cultured and intelligent, but . . . lacking in the traits which are more closely associated with forceful leadership....Those who have the scarce qualities of initiative and self-assurance tend to rise in the ranks of the profession."[1]

With the issues and problems confronting librarians for the foreseeable future, directors must be both managers and leaders. In *Leadership and Academic Librarians*, a 1998 book edited by Terrence F. Mech and Gerard B. McCabe, there is discussion of leadership as it applies to librarianship. For instance, there is mention of

- The director "as a campus leader";
- Visionary leadership with libraries;
- Transformational leadership in libraries;
- Leadership "within the ranks of academic librarians"; and
- "Reengineering-based library leadership."[2]

A comparison of the books by Morrison and by Mech and McCabe underscores a fact long known: times change—expectations of directors do not remain static. Directors of today and tomorrow play a key role external to the library.

Preparation for a position as director of an academic or public library, especially those affiliated with large, complex organizations, requires the attainment of a set of key managerial and leadership qualities—knowledge, skills, abilities, personality traits, and attributes—that enhance one's ability to perform the assigned roles and responsibilities effectively.[3] The purpose of *The Next Library Leadership* is to identify a sweeping set of qualities and then to make that list more useful. Ultimately, an institution will select directors who have those qualities it deems most essential at the time of hiring. The new director will likely want a senior management team that has complementary qualities. Thus, this book does not suggest that any one person needs to possess every quality identified. The management team, as a whole, will probably possess those qualities most essential to organizational success.

The discussion that follows should be of interest to several different audiences: (1) those directors wanting to reassess the qualities they possess, to identify new qualities to acquire, and to mentor subordinates on selected qualities; (2) those individuals with aspirations of becoming directors of academic and public libraries; (3) researchers wanting to continue our research into managerial leadership; (4) professional associations and leadership institutes wanting to highlight those qualities they can best provide and to engage in outcomes assessment showing the extent to which they have gained those qualities; and (5) students in LIS programs exploring career paths. These students should feel encouraged that they are entering a profession that offers great opportunities for career advancement. With the graying of the profession and the vast number of retirements, the "best and the brightest" among the present generation of students, as well as future ones, should find ample opportunities to seek more challenging positions and to exercise leadership within and beyond their institution. Who knows which students will eventually lead the major university and public libraries of the nation? Thus, these students, as well as recent graduates of LIS programs, need not just "dream the dream"; with the necessary support, they can make that dream a reality.

NOTES

1. Perry D. Morrison, The Career of the Academic Librarian: A Study of the Social Origins, Educational Attainments, Vocational Experience, and Personality Characteristics of a Group of American Academic Librarians (Chicago: American Library Association, 1969), 57, 58, 93.
2. Terrence F. Mech and Gerard B. McCabe, eds., Leadership and Academic Librarians (Westport, Conn.: Greenwood Press, 1998).
3. See Catherine J. Matthews, "Becoming a Chief Librarian: An Analysis of Transition Stages in Academic Library Leadership," Library Trends 50 (spring 2002): 578–602. She discusses four transition stages (preparation, encounter, adjustment, and stabilization) applicable to becoming a library director. This book fits within her preparation stage.

ACKNOWLEDGMENTS

We wish to thank those librarians who participated in our Delphi surveys as well as those who participated in the interviews and who provided written commentaries for selected chapters. We also thank Robert E. Dugan for his helpful suggestions; Kathy Sherman, administrative secretary to the dean, Northern Illinois University Libraries; and George Soete for letting us quote from his writings. Needless to say, any mistakes in this book are ours.

1

———◆•◆•◆———

A SHORTAGE OF LIBRARIANS

40% of librarians [surveyed] said they would retire in nine years or less; 68% in 14 years or less.[1]

[T]he single most important source of recruitment has been referral by professionals in the field.[2]

This chapter shows that the pool of highly qualified individuals likely to assume library directorships derives from a profession facing a severe shortage of individuals becoming librarians and remaining in the profession throughout their careers. One author discussing African American librarians noted that "these gatekeepers of African American culture, around whom many community activities revolve, are exiting the profession in droves, with few replacements in sight, and the decimation of the ranks is leaving a cultural vacuum that gets increasingly hard to fill."[3] With this national shortage, it is almost as if we could envision signs, advertisements, and commercials reading, "Help desperately wanted in our nation's libraries."[4]

NATIONAL LIBRARIAN SHORTAGE

As James M. Matarazzo, former dean of the Graduate School of Library and Information Science, Simmons College, notes, the number of librarians entering the profession cannot keep pace with the number of retirements. According to his research, many librarians retire at age sixty-three or earlier, while the number of them working past age sixty-five has decreased dramatically. Furthermore, he finds that, between 1990 and 2010, more than 83,000 librarians will have reached retirement age. Explained another way, every twenty years, half of the workforce retires. In addition, two-thirds of the librarians presently employed are between the ages of forty and sixty-four. Only 22 percent are under thirty-five, whereas 4 percent are at least sixty-five. People also leave the profession each year for reasons other than retirement (e.g., death or switching careers).

Looking at the replacement workforce, Matarazzo notes that schools of library and information studies (LIS) graduate approximately 5,000 students annually in North America. The average age of these students, he points out, is approximately thirty-five.[5] Thus, the percentage of the workforce between the ages of thirty-five and sixty-four is not likely to diminish. Clearly, an insufficient number of recent college graduates enter these schools to produce a significant change in these statistics. The shortage of librarians, especially younger ones, is unlikely to change in the near future and, as already noted, the number of those entering the profession will not be sufficient to replace the number of retirements.

Mary Jo Lynch, director of the American Library Association's Office for Research and Statistics, supports Matarazzo's conclusions. She states "that libraries—especially public libraries—are having a hard time filling positions that require the master's degree in library and information studies."[6] Based on interviews that journalists have conducted, she concludes that the "chief...reasons for the problem...[are] low salaries, competition from the private sector, and an increasing number of retirements." Based on 1990 census data, Lynch believes that the number of librarians in the country is 197,000, but "that fewer than half of...[them] had the master's degree or higher." She estimates that the number with the actual academic credentials is more than 87,000.[7] It is clear that this number fluctuates as librarians retire, leave, or enter the profession.

Articles appearing in *Career Journal,* a *Wall Street Journal* publication, and elsewhere, note a demand for special librarians able "to navigate the Internet, establish Intranets, search databases and classify information"[8] and for corporate librarians "in traditional areas, such as law and financial services, but also in fields such as executive recruiting and consulting."[9] One reporter notes that "the profession owes this boost largely to the growth of the Internet, which has caused an information explosion that must be managed."[10]

The demand for an increase in the professional workforce, however, is not limited to corporate and special libraries. It also exists in other types of libraries: school, public, and academic libraries. In many public schools, there is a dire need for teachers, with some communities in competition to hire new teachers. However, the growth in the number of teachers may not be accompanied by a similar growth in library collections and the assignment of professional librarians to manage those collections. In times of economic and fiscal entrenchment, librarians might be the first to be let go, in the belief that the number of classroom teachers must be preserved. Thus, there is a shortage of school librarians, but that shortage may not translate into a hiring demand.

As the demand for more professional staff in academic and public libraries intensifies, a larger percentage of the annual graduates of LIS programs may opt for employment in corporate libraries or for nontraditional careers (e.g., in information brokerage firms), where they perceive the starting salary as better than those offered in other types of libraries.[11] Even with the tight fiscal climate that school libraries typically face, graduates, assuming they have the necessary qualifications, may still prefer to take their chances in finding employment in a school setting. After all, salaries are linked to those of classroom teachers, which, in some communities, are higher than those for public librarians who have not been in their positions very long. Furthermore, benefits include school vacations, often including an extended summer vacation.

As a result of the shortage, libraries may be in competition with their counterparts elsewhere to attract new librarians. Furthermore, positions may go unfilled for long periods of time. Jean Porrazzo, a staff writer for *Enterprise* (in Brockton, Massachusetts), reports the concern of directors about the significant impact "if communities fail to recruit a new generation of librarians." She comments that "public libraries without qualified staff may not be eligible for state funding, which would result in fewer [library] programs, fewer resources, and reduced library hours. The shortage could hit children's programs especially hard."[12] If this were to occur, increased pressure would be placed on public library directors to cope with the stringent conditions.

There is a shortage of public librarians in rural communities with populations of less than 10,000.[13] The graduates of master's degree programs prefer to go to urban centers and organizations that offer better salaries and benefits. There is also a severe shortage of branch librarians "who can speak the languages of newcomers who live in cities."[14]

Both Lynch and Matarazzo suggest that the shortage "is likely to become more troublesome in the immediate future" and that there is need for major recruitment efforts.[15] On January 10, 2002, First Lady Laura Bush addressed the shortage by announcing a proposed $10 million initiative for 2003 to recruit a new generation of librarians. In July, the Institute of Museum and Library Services (IMLS) awarded nearly $2 million to colleges and universities in the United States for the recruitment and education of students in library and information studies. The awards also provide advanced training for librarians, especially in digital technologies.

Complicating matters, as Paula T. Kaufman of the University of Illinois at Urbana-Champaign maintains, "more librarians seem to be content to stay in their current institutions, and many librarians are uninterested in leaving their specialties to embark upon managerial paths."[16] She notes that "the challenges of recruiting new people to our profession, developing and retaining them in our institutions, and making management positions an attractive alternative to their current job" must be resolved. To do this, she favors "hiring talented people for the general areas in which we need them, and then designing jobs around them." She also advocates the use of internships, part-nerships, and development programs as "approaches for recruiting talented employees."[17]

Kaufman points out that, in the past, it was easier to entice librarians into middle management positions and to encourage them to assume greater responsibilities (e.g., those associated with senior librarians). Enticement centered on better compensation packages and on assuming more chal-lenging positions. Currently, there is less inclination for many frontline librarians to assume managerial responsibilities. They probably perceive the directorship as being too demanding of one's time and energies, and they do not see the extra salary as sufficient motivation to change their mind and lifestyle.

ACADEMIC LIBRARY DIRECTORSHIPS: IN A STATE OF FLUX?

In their classic 1973 *College & Research Libraries* article, Arthur M. McAnally and Robert B. Downs reported that "all was not well in the library directors' world." The fact that seven positions opened in one year (1971–1972), they thought, reflected a "vague feeling of uneasiness" with academic librarianship and higher education. After all, these positions were within major, national universities "whose directorships have been stable in the past" (until the 1970s, university library directors tended to stay in one position until they retired).[18]

More recently, Peter Hernon, Ronald R. Powell, and Arthur P. Young reported that, between 1994 and the end of the decade, sixty-nine individu-als became directors of libraries having membership in the Association of Research Libraries (ARL), and, from January 2000 to September 2001, twenty-five directorships of ARL university libraries became vacant, due pri-marily to retirements (60 percent).[19] Clearly, the turnover has been high and is likely to remain so in the near future.

James G. Neal, dean of Columbia University Libraries, analyzed ARL directorships from 1948 to 2002 and referred to them as "in transition." He documents that the turnover of directorships from 1998 to 2002 was due to retirement (67.7 percent), assuming the directorship of either another ARL library (13.6 percent) or a non-ARL library (3.4 percent), taking a library position at the same institution (8.5 percent), becoming a faculty member (3.4 percent), or death (3.4 percent). He also noted that the percentage of female directors increased from 22.4 percent in 1982 to 52.1 percent in 2002.[20]

Stanley Wilder, then assistant dean at the University of Rochester Libraries and author of a demographic profile of librarians, confirmed the trend when he pointed out that "the age of the ARL directors population increased dramatically from 1990 to 1998. For example, 63% of ARL university library directors were age 50 or over in 1990, compared to 91% in 1998. More to the point, 28% of these directors were age 60 or over in 1998."[21]

Three librarians from Temple University noted that "academic libraries are having a great deal of difficulty filling vacant positions at the professional, paraprofessional, and other support staff levels." "Even the pool for University Librarians/Directors," they indicated, "is getting smaller and smaller....Applicant pools often consist of only three or four people, none of whom necessarily has all of the qualifications asked for in a position description."[22] In July 2000, members of the College Library Leadership Committee, College Library Section, of the Association of College and Research Libraries, lamented "the current difficulty in finding college library directors."[23]

EMPLOYMENT OUTLOOK

According to the *Occupational Outlook Handbook 2002–03,*

Employment of librarians is expected to grow more slowly than the average for all occupations over the 2000–10 period. The increasing use of computerized information storage and retrieval systems continues to contribute to slow growth in demand for librarians. Computerized systems make cataloguing easier, which library technicians now handle. In addition, many libraries are equipped for users to access library computers directly from their home or offices. These systems allow users to bypass librarians and conduct research on their own. However, librarians are needed to manage staff, help users develop database searching techniques, address complicated reference requests, and define users' needs. Despite expectations of slower-than-average employment growth, the need to replace librarians as they retire will result in numerous additional job openings.

In discussing salaries, the same annual publication of the Department of Labor reported that "librarians with primarily administrative duties often have greater earnings. Median annual earnings of librarians in 2000 were $41,700. The middle 50 percent earned between $32,840 and $52,110. The lowest 10 percent earned less than $25,030, and the highest 10 percent earned more than $62,990."[24] It is important to note that the *Handbook*'s coverage is limited to corporate libraries. As a result, these descriptive statistics do not characterize the entire profession.

Naturally, the *Handbook*'s description of librarians and its forecast of employment opportunities speak to the recruitment of the new professional. There is no mention, however, of the place of managers and leaders in shaping a changing environment and leading a workforce to accomplish stated tasks. Moreover, the listing fails to address librarians working in school, public, and academic library environments.

CHALLENGES

"By and large, we tend to be as a profession middle-aged or a bit older, primarily Caucasian, and many of the populations we are serving are growing increasingly diverse," says Ray English, director of libraries at Oberlin College.[25] The trend is for the librarians to be older than practitioners of other professions, except for physicians and dentists, "whose lengthy internships and residencies delay their careers."[26] The reason for the older age bracket is that librarians change careers or decide to move from nonprofessional to professional status within a library. Thus, the length of time that one spends in the profession as a "professional" is likely to be less than found in most other professions. If the average graduate of a master's program is in his or her mid-thirties or forties, and if that person does not die, retire (before age sixty-five), or change careers, then the duration of that person's learning of, and contribution to, the profession may be between twenty and thirty years—less any lapses in service (e.g., to care for an aging parent, illness, or to raise children). (Note that some people may be in the profession longer, assuming they moved from paraprofessional to professional positions.)

In some instances, upon graduation from schools of library and information studies, some new librarians assume the directorship of a small academic or public library. Even for those librarians who do not become directors immediately, there is sufficient time to gain the necessary background knowledge and managerial skills to direct a small- to medium-sized academic or public library. Those making the hiring decisions increasingly want successful candidates to demonstrate a broad array of managerial leadership qualities, defined as the desired knowledge, skills, abilities, personality traits, and attributes.

The larger and more complex the organization, the more essential it is for the senior management team to possess a broad range of those qualities. Those making hiring decisions may want the successful candidate to have a specified number of years in managerial and supervisory positions (that number might range from three to ten), perhaps in different libraries. Thus, individuals may have an abbreviated career as library director, especially if they retire early or leave the profession.

Turning to university libraries within the ARL, the librarians tend to be "older than comparable professionals and even older than U.S. librarians in general, and they are aging quickly; in 1986, 42.4% of the ARL university library population was 45 or older; compare that with 48.0% in 1990, 58.0% in 1994, and 66.1% in 1998."[27] (These findings support those of Wilder—see note 21.)

Regardless of the length of time one serves as a director, it is apparent that there is mobility at the director level as people advance in their careers. For example, those assuming positions as directors of libraries within ARL come from directorships at other ARL libraries, and in their career changes they are moving to more prestigious settings. They might also come from directorships at college and non-ARL universities, positions as associate or assistant university librarians within ARL and other institutions, or from the faculties of their institutions.

Fortunately, in the past, the profession has been able to attract superior intellectual talent. The challenge is to continue to attract such talent, to create stimulating opportunities for those individuals to develop and contribute to the profession, and to nurture them for positions as managers and leaders. At the same time, another challenge will be to identify and attract a more youthful and culturally diverse talent pool. Part of that attraction must be better salaries and benefits so that these recruits will not be seduced by the corporate world, but will want to become the leaders of tomorrow within academic and public libraries. Matarazzo put the critical issue dramatically and succinctly when he said, "one way to get more people into the field...[:] Salary, salary, salary."[28]

ACUTE SHORTAGE IMPACTING THE POSITION OF DIRECTOR?

In May 2002, the Ad Hoc Task Force on Recruitment and Retention Issues, a subcommittee of the Association of College and Research Libraries, Personnel Administrators and Staff Development Officers Discussion Group, issued a white paper on "Recruitment, Retention and Restructuring: Human Resources in Academic Libraries." The findings of that report echo a number of the points already made in this chapter, namely that "librarianship is experiencing a labor gap between increasing demand for library and information science professionals and a declining supply of qualified individuals—resulting in an increasing number of unsuccessful recruitment efforts."[29] The report goes on to note that, "with the rapid rise in information technology and electronic information resources, the demand for skilled library professionals is on the increase." The "decreasing supply of qualified professionals" is due to

- The aging of the general labor supply and of the library profession, leading to an increasing number of retirements;
- One of the lowest unemployment rates in U.S. history;
- Increased competition from other career sectors (e.g., private sector, corporate libraries, technology, and dot.com companies);
- Less than competitive salaries; and
- A lingering negative image of the profession.[30]

Furthermore, "the increasing demand for library professionals coupled with the changing nature of librarianship is beginning to impact the recruitment environment, which is likely to change dramatically and become increasingly competitive. Shortages of...[LIS] degree holders, increasing retirements, and low salaries make the supply/demand gap even greater for academic libraries."[31] As well, "individual institutions...face challenges in recruiting potential candidates to their particular school or library. Factors beyond the control of the institution or library—geography or cost of living or housing or requirements for tenure, for example—can negatively impact whether or not individuals will apply."[32]

As this chapter notes, with the difficulty of filling entry-level positions, combined with fewer library and information science graduates "selecting academic libraries as their intended career path,"[33] the graying of academic librarians, and the number of people satisfied with their present position (i.e., assistant/associate/deputy librarians of university libraries [AULs]), a future crisis could be looming. The white paper calls for strategies related to "recruitment, retention [i.e., salaries, working conditions, job enrichment, and education], and the potential restructuring of library education and the library workforce,"[34] as librarianship tries to increase the number of entry-level librarians with the Master's degree in Library and Information Studies (MLIS) at a time of increased fiscal retrenchment (conceivably less money to devote to resources, human and other). Chapters 8 and 9 of this book extend the discussion by exploring ways to increase the pool of qualified individuals able and willing to assume directorships of academic and public libraries.

CONCLUSION

Clearly, a number of writers, and those they interviewed, think that there is a severe shortage of individuals entering the profession. They also note the difficulty in finding individuals with the specialized skills that some positions require and in retaining librarians who seek positions that offer higher salaries and better benefits.[35] Donald E. Riggs, vice-president for information services, University Library, Nova Southeastern University, concludes that, at present, there is no library leadership crisis. However, "if we continue to be passive, inert, and drift along without proper attention to...[leadership in the profession], the crisis will certainly occur."[36]

Against this background, some additional questions that merit consideration are

- In the future, will this situation affect the pool of those likely to become library directors?
- Upon entry into the profession, what are effective ways to continue to develop managerial and leadership qualities?
- If, indeed, there are natural-born leaders, how can they be identified, mentored, and nurtured?

Without a sufficient pool of individuals possessing the necessary qualities to assume positions of leadership, organizations will have to turn elsewhere for future leaders and directors. In some instances, positions are filled rapidly, but, in other instances, there is dissatisfaction with the pool of candidates. Positions might remain unfilled for a length of time or reopen within a couple of years. We all have a stake in identifying key qualities and ensuring that a sizeable pool of talented individuals has attained them. At the same time, will "the best and the brightest of the profession . . . continue to seek the position of director given the difficulties and pressures of the position[?]"[37] Clearly, we do not want to see a decline in the quality of directors who lead America's libraries and who represent the profession to stakeholders and constituency groups.

> Our challenge is clearly about recruitment, but it is also about diversifying our workforce.[38]

> The real management issue resulting from retirements is replacements: how can librarianship recruit new entrants to the profession in sufficient number, quality, and expertise to replace its retirees?[39]

NOTES

1. Evan St. Lifer, "The Boomer Brain Drain: The Last of a Generation," *Library Journal* 125 (May 1, 2000): 38.
2. James M. Matarazzo, "Who Wants to Be a Millionaire (Sic Librarian!)," *The Journal of Academic Librarianship* 26 (September 2000): 309.
3. Melody M. McDowell, "Help Wanted at Our Libraries," *Black Issues Book Review* 3 (March–April 2001): 78–79 (available: ProQuest: http://iibp. chadwyck.com/fulltext?ACTION=byid&ID=00033922).
4. Ibid.
5. James M. Matarazzo, unpublished paper, Simmons College, Boston, 2002. See also James M. Matarazzo, "Library Human Resources: The Y2K Plus 10 Challenge," *The Journal of Academic Librarianship* 26 (July 2000): 223–24.
6. Mary Jo Lynch, "Reaching 65: Lots of Librarians Will Be There Soon," *American Libraries* 33 (March 2002): 55.
7. Ibid.
8. Maura Rurak, "Demand Explodes for Librarians with High-tech Research Skills," *Career Journal* (from the *Wall Street Journal*) (available: http://www.careerjournal.com . . . dustries/librarians/19980825-rurak.html), accessed 1 September 2002.
9. Kelly Gates, "Librarians Are Finding Ample Opportunities," *Career Journal* (from the *Wall Street Journal*) (available: http://www.careerjournal.com . . . dustries/librarians/20001206-gates.html), accessed 1 September 2002.
10. See, for example, ibid.
11. Heather Doffing, "Extended Hours Create Shortage of Librarians," *Daily Sundial Online* (available: http://sundial.csun.edu/sun/01s/051501ne4.htm). See also Jean Porrazzo, "Librarian Shortage Looms," *The Enterprise*, Brockton, Mass., February 10, 2002 (available: http://enterprise.southofboston.com/archives). See also Ron Cromwell, dean of the

School of Education and Allied Studies, Bridgewater State University, in "Librarian Shortage Looms," *The Enterprise*, Brockton, Mass., February 10, 2002 (available: http://www.bridgew.edu/NEWSEVNT/BSCNews 1020215.html).

12. Porrazzo, "Librarian Shortage Looms."
13. Ibid.
14. Ibid.
15. Ibid.; see also Matarazzo, internal documentation.
16. Paula T. Kaufman, "Where Do the Next 'We' Come From," *ARL,* no. 221 [a bimonthly report on research library issues and actions from ARL, CNI, and SPARC, published by the Association of Research Libraries, Washington, D.C.] (April 2002): 2.
17. Ibid., 4, 3, 2.
18. Arthur M. McAnally and Robert B. Downs, "The Changing Role of Directors of University Libraries," *College & Research Libraries* 34 (March 1973): 103.
19. Peter Hernon, Ronald R. Powell, and Arthur P. Young, "University Library Directors in the Association of Research Libraries: The Next Generation: Part One," *College & Research Libraries* 62 (March 2001): 117; Peter Hernon, Ronald R. Powell, and Arthur P. Young, "University Library Directors in the Association of Research Libraries: The Next Generation: Part Two," *College & Research Libraries* 63 (January 2002): 74.
20. James G. Neal, "Turnover Trends: ARL Library Directors, 1948–2002," in *ARL Proceedings of the 141st Annual Meeting* [published by the Association of Research Libraries, Washington, D.C.] (October 2002) (available: http://www.arl.org/arl/proceedings/141/).
21. Stanley Wilder, "The Changing Profile of Research Library Professional Staff," *ARL,* nos. 208 and 209 [a bimonthly report on research library issues and actions from ARL, CNI, and SPARC, published by the Association of Research Libraries, Washington, D.C.] (February–April 2000): 3 (available: http://www.arl.org/newsltr/208–209/chgprofile.html).
22. Ivy Bayard, Carol Lang, and Maureen Pastine, "Staffing Issues for Academic Libraries," *Library Issues: Briefings for Faculty and Administrators* 22 (September 2001): 1.
23. American Library Association, Association of College and Research Libraries, College Library Leadership Committee, Committee Minutes, paper presented at annual meeting, Chicago, July 10, 2000 (available: http://www.austinc.edu/CLS/leadann00.html).
24. U.S. Department of Labor, Bureau of Labor Statistics, *Occupational Outlook Handbook 2002–03* (Washington, D.C.: GPO, 2002): 190. (available: http://stats.bls.gov/oco/ocos068.html). Additional information can be found at http://www.execpc.com/~csip/CSIP/, which is the home page of the Center for the Study of Information Professionals, Inc. The Center is a nonprofit, 501(c)(3) research and education organization, established in 1995. It offers an excellent introduction to the professions, in particular the information service professions. Also see Mary Jo Lynch, "Librarian Salaries: Annual Increase above National Average," *American Libraries* 33 (September 2002): 93.

25. Ray English as quoted in Andrea Billups, "Lack of Librarians," *Insight on the News* 16 (August 28, 2000): 24.

26. St. Lifer, "The Boomer Brain Drain," 40. See also Larry Hardesty, "The Future of Academic/Research Librarians: A Period of Transition—to What?" in *Global Issues in Twenty-First-Century Research Librarianship,* edited by Sigrún Klara Hannesdóttir (Helsinki, Finland: NORDINFO, 2002), 576–601.

27. Wilder, "The Changing Profile of Research Library Professional Staff," 1. See also Stanley Wilder, "The Age Demographics of Academic Librarians: A Profession Apart," *Journal of Library Administration* 28, no. 3 (1999): 1–84.

28. James M. Matarazzo as quoted in St. Lifer, "The Boomer Brain Drain," 41.

29. Association of College and Research Libraries, Personnel Administrators and Staff Development Officers Discussion Group, Ad Hoc Task Force on Recruitment and Retention Issues Group, "Recruitment, Retention and Restructuring: Human Resources in Academic Libraries" (Chicago: American Library Association, Association of College and Research Libraries, May 2002), 4 (available: http://www.ala.org/acrl/recruit-wp.html).

30. Ibid.

31. Ibid.

32. Ibid., 14.

33. Ibid., 14–15.

34. Ibid., 4.

35. See also Jennifer Jacobson, "A Shortage of Academic Librarians," *The Chronicle of Higher Education: Career Network* (August 14, 2002) (available: http://chronicle.com/jobs/2002/08/200208/40/c.htm).

36. Donald E. Riggs, "The Crisis and Opportunities in Library Leadership," *Journal of Library Administration*™ 32, nos. 3 and 4 (2001): 16.

37. Dana C. Rooks, "Terms for Academic Library Directors," *Library Trends* 43 (summer 1994): 59.

38. John W. Berry, "Addressing the Recruitment and Diversity Crisis (President's Message)," *American Libraries* 33 (February 2002): 7.

39. Stanley J. Wilder, "New Hires in Research Libraries: Demographic Trends and Hiring Priorities," in *ARL,* no. 221 [a bimonthly report on research library issues and actions from ARL, CNI, and SPARC, published by the Association of Research Libraries, Washington, D.C.] (April 2002): 5.

2

QUALITIES EXPECTED OF LIBRARY DIRECTORS: A REVIEW OF THE LITERATURE

Many forces are changing the landscape of higher education, and libraries are certainly feeling their brunt.[1]

A. J. Anderson, professor emeritus at Simmons College and author of a noted and long-running column on management appearing in *Library Journal,* distinguishes between management and leadership. "The main aim of managers," he notes, "is to maximize the output of the organization through administrative implementation. To achieve this, they must undertake the following *functions:* planning, organizing, leading, controlling, and implementing." He continues,

In order to function effectively, a manager must develop technical, human, and conceptual skills; focus on the growth and use of information processing and communication technology; maintain an effective and representative governance system to guide the mission of the organization; develop policies and procedures to ensure compliance with local, state, and federal laws; demand the highest standards of self and others, leading by example through maintaining the highest degree of personal integrity and professional ethics; and be a leader capable of achieving organizational goals and mission.

Leadership is one component of the functions of management . . . [; it] is the process of influencing (and interacting with) others to attain group, organizational, and societal goals. The central attribute is *social influence.* An old adage maintains that "leaders lead people, managers manage things." Leadership skills development requires investment in difficult areas like people skills, personal development, and an unending mental flexibility to tolerate extra-rational and emotional human complexity. Leaders must know how to mentor, coach others, give presentations, and practice listening, sharing, and facilitating.[2]

Murray Hiebert and Bruce Klatt's *Encyclopedia of Leadership* is an excellent resource for information on topics such as tools for strategic thinking, designing productive processes, problem-solving techniques, initiating and leading teams and groups, optimizing meetings, and much more.[3] There is also much to be learned in Robert M. Fulmer and Marshall Goldsmith's *Leadership Investment,* which explains how major corporations achieve strategic advantage through leadership development.[4] Anyone contemplating in-house management development programs should consult William J. Rothwell and H. C. Kazanas's *Building In-house Leadership and Management Development Programs.*[5]

As some authors writing in the 1990s looked to the unfolding of the new millennium, one of the questions they raised was, "What qualities will future leaders of the library and other professions need to possess?" This question is central to this chapter and the research reported in the following chapters.

Although there have been numerous studies of leadership traits, there is little overlap among those traits identified—"only 5 percent of the [same] traits were found in four or more studies," according to Robert D. Stueart and Barbara B. Moran. They conclude that "there is no such thing as a single leader type. Instead, there is much variation in the skills, abilities, and personalities of successful leaders,"[6] and, we would add, of successful managers. Thus, this chapter does not attempt to compile a comprehensive list of the qualities identified in the literatures of different disciplines, fields, and professions. Clearly, the lists provided in this chapter and in subsequent chapters are not intended as definitive and representative of all styles of leadership. Further, it is not our intention to identify statistical relationships or differences. Rather, our purpose is to guide future leaders and directors, as well as those hiring them, in ascertaining qualities—knowledge, skills, abilities, and personality traits—that those participating in the research for this book perceive as important (but not necessarily as all inclusive) for the present and next decades.

The rest of this chapter focuses on academic and public libraries and does not address other types of libraries, except for a brief section on medical libraries; other types are outside the scope of this book and the research reported in it. Furthermore, given the extensive literature on leadership, including leadership fads, the discussion of these writings is limited but still representative of the literature.

LEADERSHIP QUALITIES

As researchers Robert J. House and Ram N. Aditya note,

[Although the phenomenon of leadership has been around since antiquity,] the social scientific study of leadership started in the early 1930s. Over the years, the cultivation of knowledge about this phenomenon has been cumulative. Trait, behavioral, contingency and neo-charismatic paradigms have contributed to the development of leadership studies.

Yet, as they observe, there are still "deficiencies" in the research on leadership. These deficiencies, which they proceed to analyze, relate, for instance, to "leadership styles," "diversity management," "strategic leadership," "management training and development," and "universal or near universal effective leader behaviors."[7] Nonetheless, scholars have continued to identify new qualities and expand on skill sets already known.

Several researchers, including Allen J. Morrison, Margaret E. Alldredge, and Kevin J. Nilan, focus on the development of leadership competencies that are specific to an organization. These competencies address unique organizational requirements and strategies, and they impact on the leadership needs of the organization.[8]

Daniel Goleman, cochairman of the Consortium for Research on Emotional Intelligence in Organizations (based at Rutgers University's Graduate School of Applied Psychology), identifies six leadership styles (see Table 2.1) and maintains that effective leaders do not limit themselves to any one style; different circumstances call for different styles.[9]

Table 2.1
Leadership Styles

	Coercive	Authoritative	Affiliative	Democratic	Pacesetting	Coaching
The leader's modus operandi	Demands immediate compliance	Mobilizes people toward a vision	Creates emotional bonds and harmony	Forges consensus through participation	Expects excellence and demonstrates self-direction	Develops people for the future
The style in a phrase	"Do what I say"	"Come with me"	"People come first"	"What do you think?"	"Do as I do and do it now"	"Try this"
Underlying emotional intelligence competencies	Drive to achieve, initiative, self-control	Self-confidence, empathy, change catalyst	Empathy, building relationships, communication creates loyalty	Collaboration, team leadership, communication	Conscientiousness, drive to achieve, initiative	Developing others, empathy, self-awareness
When the style works best	In a crisis, to kick-start a turn-around, or with problem employees	When changes require a new vision, or when a clear direction is needed	To heal rifts in a team or to motivate people during stressful circumstances	To build buy-in or consensus, or to get input from valuable employees	To get quick results from a highly motivated and competent team	To help an employee improve performance or develop long-term strengths
Effect on climate and result	Negative	Most strongly positive	Positive	Positive	Negative	Positive

Source: Reprinted by permission of *Harvard Business Review.* From "Leadership That Gets Results," by Daniel Goleman, *Harvard Business Review* 78 (March 2000): 78–90. Copyright © 2000 by the Harvard Business School Publishing Corporation; all rights reserved.

Aspects of leadership relate to managing and shaping change, as well as being able to articulate necessary changes and to rally the organization around the accomplishment of change—crucial to achievement of the organization's mission, goals, and objectives. F. Kramer, a consultant and business leader, summarizes nicely the steps for initiating and accomplishing change: analyze the organization's need for change; work to build a vision and common direction; create a sense of urgency (but do not panic); put a strong leader in charge of the effort; generate a broad base of support for the program; create a plan for implementing the change; develop programs to help employees contribute to, and accept, the change; be communicative and honest; and reinforce the change and institutionalize it.[10]

A perusal of the literature on leadership, regardless of discipline, suggests that essential traits include: integrity, setting an example, striving for self-improvement, loyalty, maturity, good listening skills, achievable vision, adaptability, effective interpersonal communication, perseverance, self-discipline, flexibility, confidence, endurance, people orientation, decisiveness, compassion, taking initiative, coolness under stress, energy and energizing others, mental and physical stamina, and so forth. Hap Klopp and Tracy B. Klopp, authors of *The Adventure of Leadership,* maintain that great leaders have the following tangible and intangible attributes: an ability to act on intuition and to make tough decisions, a global perspective, an appreciation for diversity, a sense of urgency, and an ability to deal with those they do not control.[11] *Why the Best Man for the Job Is a Woman* emphasizes that leaders sell the vision of the organization, reinvent the rules, concentrate on achievement, demonstrate "courage under fire," convert challenges into opportunities, have an acute awareness of customer preferences, and "maximize high touch in an era of high tech."[12] Writer Robert Barner emphasizes adaptability, effective interpersonal communication, and good decision making.[13]

Writing for the American Management Association, Warren Blank identifies a large number of skills as essential for leaders to possess. Among these are building rapport and trust; exerting "influence across, down, and outside the organization"; "creating a motivating environment"; "demonstrating rock-solid integrity"; creating "mutually agreed-on and shared expectations"; forging alliances; working through resistance; fostering open communication; and reframing messages to motivate others.[14]

A collection of essays published in 1990, *Developing Leadership Skills: A Source Book for Librarians,* identifies a number of leadership qualities, including, for instance, self-esteem, intuition, interpersonal communication skills, effective time management, relevant values and ethics, the ability to handle stress, and managerial delegation.[15] Jo Ellen Misakian, a school media center specialist, believes that leadership centers around passion for one's work, persistence, perceptiveness, persuasiveness, policy acumen, a positive attitude, being practical and a problem-solver, being professional and progressive (visionary), being productive, and being involved (a participant).[16] However, she does not explain how each quality applies to leadership; some pertain more to being a good professional.

It merits mention that a combined issue of the *Journal of Library Administration*™ is devoted to "Leadership in the Library and Information Science Professions: Theory and Practice."[17] The papers add to the list of qualities identified in this section and subsequent ones. Becky Schreiber and John Shannon, partners in Schreiber Shannon Associates, for instance, identified "six critical leadership traits": "self-awareness," "embracing change," "customer focus," "a shared vision to pull the organization into the future," "collaborative spirit," and "bias for courageous action."[18] Camila A. Alire, then dean of the libraries, Colorado State University, lists "leadership qualities, traits, and skills," and categorizes the items on the list into "charismatic, visionary, personal, organizational, and leadership development." She believes that these qualities "are particularly relative to guiding emerging library leaders of color, with the intent of diversifying the leadership box of crayons."[19]

The home pages of leadership institutes suggest other qualities relating to leadership. The ACRL (Association of College and Research Libraries)/Harvard Leadership Institute of Harvard University's Graduate School of Education (http://www.gse.harvard.edu/~ppe/programs/acrl/program.html), for instance, discusses issues such as building "an effective, cohesive leadership team," the accomplishment of the institution's mission in a changing environment, the alignment of operations and resources to achieve desired results, the workplace as a setting for personal and professional growth, and the roles and responsibilities of directors in planning initiatives.

In an editorial appearing in *College & Research Libraries,* editor Donald E. Riggs views participation in scholarship as a leadership quality—one that is lacking in many academic library directors, including those in the Association of Research Libraries (ARL). The common reason (or excuse), he notes, for not engaging in scholarship is a lack of time; other activities (e.g., fundraising) consume the directors' time. As Riggs points out, library directors are not likely to gain their positions through scholarship; rather, they do so through their administrative ability. He believes that "the lack of the doctorate and a respectable scholarly record creates a situation where the teaching faculty, deans, provosts/vice presidents for academic affairs, and presidents do not perceive the library director as a fellow academician. This is especially true in institutions where library directors/deans are supposedly on par with the academic deans."[20]

Finally, this chapter's Appendix reprints a set of qualities that apply to public library directors as well as senior management teams. More than likely, one person will not possess and demonstrate command of each quality. Most impressive is the fact that this is the most detailed set of qualities discovered during the literature review.

Academic Libraries

Richard T. Sweeney of Polytechnic University (Brooklyn, New York) lists ten leadership strategies, each of which reveals some leadership qualities.[21] Mark D. Winston, assistant professor in the School of Communication, Information and Library Studies, Rutgers University, and Lisa Dunkley, manager of special projects, Rare Books and Special Collections, Princeton University Library, underscore the importance of development and fundraising as part of a director's knowledge base and skill set.[22] An excellent source for identifying other qualities is *Leadership and Academic Librarians,* edited by Terrence F. Mech and Gerard B. McCabe.[23] This source has an excellent bibliography.

As Ruth J. Person, then associate vice-chancellor for academic affairs of the University of Missouri, St. Louis, and coauthor George C. Newman, of the State University College of New York in Buffalo, point out, the director balances internal and external demands, manages innovation, maintains visibility in the professional community, and serves as a campus leader, especially during times of change. The director also has appropriate academic credentials and draws upon a wide variety of work experiences in different settings.[24]

Joanne R. Euster, former university librarian at Rutgers University, provides an excellent background to the research literature on leadership and to key leadership qualities. She produced a model, the Leader Activity Model, which views the director "as the principle source of influence directed toward the external environment" and considers the "reputational effectiveness" of this leader. She then created a profile of leadership styles that included reputational effectiveness, organizational change, and leader activity.[25]

Brooke E. Sheldon, currently dean of the School of Information Resources and Library Science, University of Arizona, compiled a collection of comments from a number of leaders in different libraries and schools of library and information studies. Among the qualities highlighted are creating and maintaining a shared vision, good communication skills, trust, self-confidence, and a willingness to engage in mentoring.[26]

Public Libraries

Patrick M. O'Brien, director of the Dallas Public Library, believes that leaders must view libraries as "service institutions," "must recognize our values as an established institution, but more importantly they must believe that we are the best at what we do and will be the best at anything we undertake."[27] They must also be people oriented. Noting that "a common thread" in the definitions of leadership is "humanness," he maintains that leaders "must have vision; must have trust and be trusted; must listen; must share power; and must have tolerance and understanding."[28] He equates power sharing with empowerment. Herbert Goldhor, professor emeritus of the University of Illinois at Urbana–Champaign, would add "a personal philosophy of librarianship," "commitment to principle," and a "strategic plan for the future development of the library."[29]

Donald J. Sager, publisher of Highsmith Press and past president of the Public Library Association, regards risk taking as a "virtue" and concludes that "what more libraries need is a risk taker."[30] Joey (Eleanor Jo) Rodger, president of the Urban Libraries Council, discusses "clusters of behavior...[that] are more related to the management roles of library directors than to their leadership roles." Nonetheless, her interviews with those involved in literacy programs revealed some leadership qualities and showed that leadership is not limited to those serving as directors.[31]

As Laurence Corbus, president of Corbus Library Consultants in Chesterland, Ohio, maintains, "a director must inspire confidence in at least three groups—the board of trustees, the staff, and the public." Furthermore, that person needs a vision of the library's role in the community, must "inspire confidence in that vision," and must also be resourceful, a team player, accountable, a people person, politically savvy, able to exercise good judgment, an entrepreneur, and a consensus builder. The director's "appearance, presentation, and approach" must be appropriate. Depending on the particular organization, a successful candidate (the new director) must be a "quick study," a "deliberate thinker," or someone in between these two positions. Corbus also notes that "formal education is a basic requirement, not a measuring stick."[32]

MANAGERIAL QUALITIES

R. Alec Mackenzie, writing in the *Harvard Business Review*, offers a graphic representation of the five functions of management recounted by Anderson. Mackenzie shows their interconnection to conceptual thinking, administration, and leadership, and, more broadly, to three elements: ideas, things, and people. Thus, he provides an extensive listing of managerial and leadership qualities.[33]

"Changes in the actual jobs of librarians and the requirements for those jobs influence change in organizational structures."[34] Clearly, directors must be aware of the changing nature of library work and recognize that changes now appear in entry-level jobs where the environments are increasingly team based. Staff members must both possess and demonstrate qualities such as effective communication and interpersonal skills, a commitment to service, an ability to work effectively with constituent groups, collegiality, creativity, enthusiasm and an outgoing personality, and flexibility.[35]

Academic Libraries

Dana C. Rooks, of the University of Houston Libraries, believes that "some of the most significant...[qualities] include" management, technical, human relations, and legal skills.[36] Sharon J. Rodgers, assistant vice-president for academic affairs and university librarian at George Washington University, together with Ruth J. Person, discussed in 1991 the recruitment of an academic library director. They grouped "preferred qualities" into "administrative experience," "education," "academic and service credentials," and "specific skills related to institutional needs." Although those skills "may vary widely from place to place," they might relate to "technical expertise in library automation and information technology, conflict-management skills, research or teaching experience, design/construction experience, fundraising abilities, . . . [and] political knowledge."[37]

Public Libraries

Goldhor distinguishes between internal administration and representing the library to its stakeholders and constituents, as well as to the library profession. Internal administration involves "maximizing the library's effectiveness . . . and its efficiency."[38] Sager emphasizes good people, communication, collaboration, customer service, and technical and marketing skills. As well, a director needs proven problem-solving ability.[39] This chapter's Appendix identifies additional qualities.

In 1983, Darlene E. Weingand, of the library school at the University of Wisconsin–Madison, and Noel Ryan, of the Mississauga Library System in Ontario, Canada, conducted a survey of top administrators, their deputies, and board chairpersons of selected U.S. and Canadian public libraries to see if the administrators and their deputies have acquired certain competencies and skills. Their survey probed fifteen managerial competences, showing the abilities to

1. Formulate policies that clearly convey the mission/philosophy of the organization, including areas of social responsibility;

2. Formulate and operate with a personal philosophy of administration;

3. Perform operational (short-term) and strategic (long-term) planning;

4. Work effectively with staff and involve them in the planning process;

5. Delegate both responsibility and authority as appropriate;

6. Determine the priorities of the organization and continually monitor and evaluate organizational effectiveness and self-renewal;

7. Develop and use instruments and procedures for assessing the needs of the community;

8. Involve the community in the planning process;

9. Select, supervise, and provide for staff development and continuing education opportunities;

10. Evaluate staff performance;

11. Exercise budgetary planning and control effectively;

12. Identify and submit realistic proposals to a variety of funding sources;

13. Experiment and take risks;

14. Utilize existing resources effectively; and

15. Monitor and analyze current trends, involving the library where appropriate.

The fifteen traits actually tend to relate to leadership more than they do to management. Nonetheless, Weingand and Ryan offer an excellent overview of the competencies recognized at the time. To the qualities already listed in this chapter, they added the following managerial skills: leading, communicating, planning, creativity, setting goals, organizing, delegating, budgeting, directing, judgment, decision making, analyzing, controlling, evaluation, training, motivating, counseling, and strategic planning.[40]

PERSONAL QUALITIES

Leadership qualities, such as integrity, are also personal qualities—related to an individual's code of ethics, behavior, value system, and personal beliefs.

Academic Libraries

Among the qualities that ARL directors believe important for the next generation are honesty, resiliency, intelligence, intuition, optimism, and enthusiasm, as well as others that we identified in our previous research and included in Table 3.1.[41] Euster identified some demographic and professional characteristics of the directors in her study population. Those characteristics centered on the habits and practices of the directors; for example, she quantified the number of professional journals scanned at least every other issue.[42]

Public Libraries

Reflecting on the position of head librarian, Goldhor wrote that many of the desired attributes "can be learned or acquired by anyone who puts his mind to it, but some come out of and flow from the individual's character, personality, and life philosophy."[43] Among the attributes he identifies are the following: have wide knowledge; willingness to engage in "continuing study of the experiences of other libraries"; knowledgeable about library literature, the literature of public and business administration, and that of related disciplines; "engage in time management"; are able to "be innovative"; pay "attention to the quality and strengths of the people who work directly with" the head librarian; are able to "tackle the hard problems and decisions"; "motivate and inspire colleagues"; are able to "work harmoniously with the board of trustees and to present the library to local government officials, to the general public, and to the library profession"; "benefit from criticism and seek regularly to secure work evaluations from the board, colleagues on the staff, and the community"; select "competent people for the necessary tasks and...arrange things so that they can perform at the highest level of their ability"; and are willing to participate in professional associations.[44] By surrounding himself or herself with high-quality people, the head librarian tries to ensure that, when he or she is away, the library functions smoothly. Goldhor also sees "these colleagues...as well known in the profession as...[the head librarian] is."[45] To Goldhor's list, Sager adds the ability to engage in self-renewal, thereby avoiding administrative burnout.[46] Again, this chapter's Appendix identifies complementary qualities.

KNOWLEDGE AREAS

Eileen McElrath, assistant professor at Valdosta State University, examined the perceptions of academic library directors and the chief academic officers to whom they report regarding the challenges libraries face. Those challenges were then grouped into the following categories: "staffing issues," "technology," "library's role," and "miscellaneous." Among the challenges were knowledge areas (e.g., fundraising) and issues related to restraining library budgets, satisfying users, and ensuring cultural diversity in the work force.[47]

Perusal of the home page for the Association of Research Libraries (ARL) (http://www.arl.org/) discloses a number of resources that identify general areas of knowledge for directors. These areas, for instance, include scholarly communication, preservation of research resources, measurement (e.g., the use of e-metrics), intellectual property rights, the impact of serial costs on library collections, the management of networked information services, and distance education. In the section on "Key Results Areas—Library Director," this chapter's Appendix identifies knowledge areas for public library directors.

QUALITIES FOR MEDICAL LIBRARIANS

To illustrate that the picture of academic and public librarianship presented in this chapter applies to special settings, it merits noting that, at its 2002 annual conference in Dallas, Texas, the Medical Library Association held a program on "developing a strategic agenda for leadership in health sciences libraries." Suspecting a shortage of capable leaders to guide these libraries in the future, conference organizers wanted to identify the key management and leadership qualities, and to encourage the association to find solutions so that a crisis does not result. The speakers and the audience divided into groups and identified qualities such as "build consensus for a shared vision," "create buy-in to that vision," "be an advocate for the library," "maintain credibility," "engender trust and confidence," "have integrity and command respect," "be honest," "be a risk taker," "learn from mistakes," "recognize weaknesses and admit them," "let employees also be leaders," "manage the grapevine," "be collaborative," "work well with others," "exercise self-discipline," "be environmentally aware (be political)," "be articulate," "create partnerships and alliances," "be a change agent," "engage in fund-raising," "be adept at time management," "be ready for change—accept change," "be able to live with uncertainty," "think outside the box," "like to work with people," "be comfortable with ambiguity," and "engage in mentoring."[48] Because Table 3.1 provided a partial foundation for the groups' discussion, it is not surprising that the list overlaps with that table. The qualities identified clearly apply to different library settings.

CONCLUSION

"There are at least 100 definitions of leadership," according to Riggs, and "the definitions include leadership styles, functional leadership, situational leadership, bureaucratic leadership, charismatic leadership, servant leadership, follower leadership, group-centered leadership, and so on."[49] Servant leadership, for instance, views service as the highest priority of the organization, and it promotes a sense of community, nurtures employees professionally, and concentrates on a passion for meeting customer expectations. Some of the more highly prized qualities of such leaders are good listening, communication, and decision-making skills; an ability to achieve the organization's mission; articulation of a realistic vision; reliance on persuasion to achieve organizational goals; open-mindedness; warmth; self-awareness; and keeping commitments.[50]

The servant-leadership style involves personal growth, but it is not an end unto itself. Rather, the style provides a foundation upon which to build other leadership styles, and recognizes that the staff holds the library in trust for the greater good of the parent institution and society.

> Libraries must take the initiative in this changing environment and use the broadest definition of our professional knowledge and services to forge a new flexible and collaborative role on campus.[51]

APPENDIX: COMPETENCIES AND RESPONSIBILITIES OF TOP MANAGEMENT TEAMS IN PUBLIC LIBRARIES

1. Leadership Abilities and Attitudes: Taking initiative, making things happen through the effective action of others.

Appendix reprinted with the permission of the Minnesota Department of Children, Families and Learning, Information Technologies/Library Development and Services Division. From Suzanne H. Mahmoodi and Geraldine King, "Identifying Competencies and Responsibilities of Top Management Teams in Public Libraries," *Minnesota Libraries* 30 (autumn–winter 1991–92): 27–32. Directors are part of the top management teams.

Vision–Future

1.1 Takes initiative to accomplish something, such as identifying and solving problems, overcoming obstacles, achieving goals, pursuing opportunities, doing things better.

1.2 Establishes and maintains an organizational culture that encourages staff to develop their maximum potential.

1.3 Recognizes changes in the economic and political environment that mandate change in the library.

1.4 Initiates, implements, and manages change.

1.5 Develops original and successful approaches (e.g., is innovative).

1.6 Develops a shared vision that builds on the past and present of public library service and looks to the future.

1.7 Understands and promotes the library's role within the larger governmental organization.

Develops Staff

1.8 Coordinates activities of individuals and groups toward accomplishment of meaningful goals.

1.9 Ensures that activities are provided to prepare staff for management functions using appropriate techniques such as coaching, counseling, and shared responsibility teams.

1.10 Establishes a staff development program.

1.11 Demonstrates respect, confidence, and trust in employees by allowing them to fulfill responsibilities with little or no intervention.

1.12 Values and respects ideas of others.

1.13 Encourages creativity and supports risk taking.

1.14 Accepts or shares responsibility as appropriate.

1.15 Uses appropriate leadership and interpersonal styles to guide individuals and groups effectively toward task accomplishment.

1.16 Creates an environment in which staff are committed to service concepts and policies and are recognized for accomplishing services and goals.

1.17 Recognizes and uses the attitudes, behavioral styles, and personal traits of others to build a work team.

1.18 Organizes activities for staff to learn and practice a variety of group process techniques such as building teams, managing projects, and conducting meetings.

2. Administrative Abilities: Structuring one's own activities and those of others; coordinating the use of resources to maximize productivity and efficiency.

Personnel

2.1 Selects the best-qualified applicant for the job.

2.2 Evaluates regularly the performance, skills, knowledge, and potential of employees based on standards.

2.3 Uses constructive feedback to improve or maintain performance.

2.4 Terminates employees based on objective performance criteria.

2.5 Serves as a buffer between those in positions above and below one's own organizational level.

2.6 Develops and administers personnel policies and procedures.

2.7 Deals with personnel consistently and fairly.

2.8 Interprets local, state, and national laws and regulations concerning personnel (e.g., workers' compensation, equal employment opportunity, social security, retirement plans).

Planning and Budgeting

2.9 Uses appropriate planning techniques.

2.10 Develops and communicates mission, roles, and functions of the library.

2.11 Develops library services appropriate to the community.

2.12 Sets challenging yet achievable goals and objectives.

2.13 Develops and communicates written policies.

2.14 Understands taxes and funding for public libraries.

2.15 Uses cost-analysis techniques.

2.16 Prepares a budget to implement the goals and objectives of an organization.

2.17 Negotiates and defends budgets with funding authorities.

2.18 Selects appropriate strategies and techniques based on priorities to meet budget constraints or changes in funding.

Operations

2.19 Recognizes the need for change in organizational structure.

2.20 Implements plans and organizational changes.

2.21 Develops strategies, tasks, and schedules to meet goals and objectives.

2.22 Sets organizational priorities.

2.23 Selects management structure appropriate to the activity.

2.24 Allocates resources (material, financial, personnel).

2.25 Administers a program within a budget.

2.26 Integrates external policies and administrative regulations (e.g., A.D.A., civil service).

2.27 Develops contract specifications and monitors contract compliance.

2.28 Plans, conducts, and participates in meetings so that the collective resources of the group members are used efficiently and effectively.

2.29 Committed to meeting performance standards (e.g., output, service, individual).

2.30 Assures that good and timely decisions are made at the appropriate level.

3. Knowledge and Skills Specific to Public Libraries and Their Role in Society: Applying the technical knowledge and political skills needed to do the job, including competence in library and information management, familiarity with information policies and practices, and including political skills for integrating the library with other appropriate organizations and dealing successfully with political and governmental officials.

   3.1 Is committed to the mission and direction of public library service.

   3.2 Is committed to intellectual freedom.

   3.3 Is committed to guaranteeing access to information for all people.

   3.4 Understands the basic technical functions of public librarianship (e.g., reference service, cataloging, collection development).

   3.5 Has basic knowledge of the technologies that have impact on library operations and services.

   3.6 Has knowledge of the historical development and trends in libraries and can relate this information to present situations and future planning.

   3.7 Has knowledge of the history and philosophy of the public library movement, including the legal basis for and laws and regulations affecting public libraries.

   3.8 Understands the roles and responsibilities of library board members and develops the board to make effective decisions in policy, planning, and financial issues.

   3.9 Keeps up-to-date with conditions, developments, and future trends in the library and information field.

3.10 Understands the resources available via state, national, and international library networks.

3.11 Understands and is able to use social science research methods to support the decision-making process.

3.12 Participates in professional activities and associations by attending meetings, conferences, educational activities, etc.; by reading professional literature; and by being active in state and national professional associations.

3.13 Is committed to one's own professional growth and development (i.e., establishes career goals that maximize personal productivity and fulfillment and builds on strengths and minimize weaknesses).

Political / Negotiating Skills

3.14 Lobbies effectively for libraries with national, state, and local officials.

3.15 Establishes cooperative working relationships with local government departments.

3.16 Develops and maintains cooperative working relationships with government officials.

3.17 Prepares the library board for its role in representing the library and lobbying.

3.18 Negotiates and maintains effective relations with unions.

3.19 Understands accountability to the general public (i.e., taxpayers).

3.20 Relates library needs and goals to those of funding officials and agencies.

3.21 Understands various organizational structures, funding, and governing patterns.

3.22 Recognizes decision-making patterns and authority.

3.23 Negotiates the best possible resources for the library in a given situation.

Community Involvement

3.24 Is committed to public service, including a commitment for the library to share, cooperate, and collaborate with other educational, cultural, and social agencies serving the community.

3.25 Is committed to planning and implementing library services based on the needs of people of diverse backgrounds and interests.

3.26 Understands the flow, use, and value of information in society as a whole and relates this to the role of libraries.

3.27 Recognizes and articulates common interests among diverse organizations and agencies.

3.28 Recognizes connections for libraries with other organizations and
agencies and capitalizes on them.

3.29 Articulates to staff the need and ways to be involved in the community.

3.30 Represents the library enthusiastically to the community.

Fundraising Skills

3.31 Articulates a vision of the library to prospective donors.

3.32 Utilizes fundraising principles and techniques.

3.33 Has effective public relations skills to pursue funding actively.

3.34 Involves staff effectively in fundraising.

3.35 Develops a strategic fundraising plan.

3.36 Uses Friends of the Library effectively in fundraising efforts.

3.37 Develops and writes proposals for state, local, federal, and private
funds.

4. Cognitive Skills/Abilities: Processing information effectively to learn new
material, identify and define problems, and make decisions. How a person
thinks and analyzes.

    4.1 Recognizes and utilizes own learning and problem-solving styles.

    4.2 Learns quickly.

    4.3 Uses complex and abstract concepts and recognizes subtle relation-
ships and new patterns in information.

    4.4 Anticipates and identifies problems, their possible causes, and alter-
native strategies or solutions.

    4.5 Works with ambiguous situations.

    4.6 Draws accurate conclusions from financial, statistical, and numerical
materials.

    4.7 Uses mathematical and statistical techniques to manipulate data.

    4.8 Defines parameters of and undertakes risks.

    4.9 Organizes systems and functions in a logical manner.

    4.10 Makes decisions, on a day-to-day basis, within the framework of the
organizational mission, goals, and objectives.

5. Interpersonal Abilities: Interacting with Others.

    5.1 Demonstrates confidence in self and others.

    5.2 Is persuasive.

5.3   Uses negotiating techniques appropriate to the situation (e.g., one-on-one, vendor, union).

5.4   Develops and maintains cooperative working relationships with staff.

5.5   Establishes trusting relationships with staff members.

5.6   Has credibility with staff.

5.7   Is supportive of organizational policies.

5.8   Deals with patron satisfaction/dissatisfaction regarding library services, procedures, and policies.

5.9   Confronts and manages conflict.

5.10 Informs others of decisions, changes, and other relevant information in a timely fashion.

5.11 Speaks effectively one-to-one, within groups, and in presentation to groups.

5.12 Uses interviewing techniques.

5.13 Listens effectively (i.e., demonstrates attention to, conveys understanding of, and comments or questions).

5.14 Writes clearly and effectively.

5.15 Creates or develops an atmosphere that supports open communication among staff members.

5.16 Is aware of how one's own behavior affects others.

6. Personal Traits.

6.1   Allocates one's own time efficiently.

6.2   Handles detail effectively and efficiently.

6.3   Is adaptable (i.e., responds appropriately and confidently to the demands of work challenges when confronted with changes, ambiguity, adversity, or other pressures).

6.4   Is change oriented (i.e., recognizes the need to change, initiates and plans change, interacts with change, or reacts to change, as appropriate).

6.5   Has self-control (i.e., is able to remain calm in stressful situations).

6.6   Meets the demands of work while managing physical and emotional stress.

6.7   Is empathetic with ideas and feelings of others.

6.8   Is self-confident.

6.9   Counsels staff to use techniques to lessen the negative effects of stress.

6.10 Acts independently or accepts direction as appropriate.

6.11 Is persistent.

6.12 Is committed to high professional and service standards.

6.13 Is committed to ethical standards.

6.14 Is committed to management of libraries and to the library profession (i.e., sees work as a central figure of life, seeks self-improvement as needed preparation for career growth, and keeps up-to-date on principles of library science, management, and organizational behavior).

6.15 Has a sense of humor.

6.16 Has integrity.

6.17 Exhibits optimism, energy, and enthusiasm.

KEY RESULTS AREAS—LIBRARY DIRECTOR

1. Fiscal management

   - Prepare budgets: annual, operating, facilities
   - Monitor and control expenditures
   - Be responsible for business operations of library: purchasing, risk management, contracts for services, etc.

2. Long-range, short-range, and strategic planning

   - Maintain planning cycle
   - Monitor progress
   - Coordinate planning efforts of staff and board
   - Develop vision

3. Personnel management and development

   - Oversee human resources program
   - Ensure compliance with local, state, and federal laws
   - Ensure opportunities for development

4. Board relations and development

   - Prepare documents for board: reports, draft agreements, requests for action, policies, etc.
   - Make recommendations for action
   - Implement decisions of board
   - Provide learning opportunities to develop boards as effective decision makers

5. Community involvement and representing library (marketing)

- Increase visibility of library
- Participate in meetings and activities of organizations within the community
- Represent library with other governmental units and boards
- Participate in professional organizations and the local professional community
- Maintain relations with Friends of the Library and other volunteer groups

6. Fundraising

- Be involved in fundraising efforts and in exploring alternate funding sources
- Develop a strategic fundraising plan
- Develop proposals for state, local, federal, and private funds

7. Program and service design, coordination, evaluation

- Ensure that library materials and services provided meet needs of communities
- Integrate program design with planning
- Ensure evaluation of services and programs
- Be responsible for reports to various governmental units
- Ensure library units are coordinated to provide maximum communications and productivity

8. Work environment (organizational structure, operations, culture)

- Organize library into operational units
- Provide atmosphere that encourages openness, trust, cooperation, and participation
- Articulate, support, and promote organizational values and vision, including innovation, trust, staff participation, and team management

9. Management of facilities and technology

- Direct facilities projects and building programs
- Plan and coordinate maintenance and improvement of library facilities and property
- Ensure libraries are easily accessed and safe
- Ensure effective use of technology

10. Personal and professional development

- Allocate one's own time efficiently
- Handle detail effectively and efficiently
- Respond appropriately and confidently to the demands of work challenges when confronted with change, ambiguity, adversity, etc.
- Establish career and nonwork goals that maximize personal productivity and fulfillment and that build on strengths and minimize weaknesses.

NOTES

1. Paula T. Kaufman [University of Illinois at Urbana–Champaign], "Thoughts of Other Academic Library Directors," *Library Cultures Exploring Dimensions of Change: A Series of Lectures and Panels* (Ann Arbor, Mich.: University of Michigan, School of Information, n.d.) (available: http://www.si.umich.edu/library-cultures/academic/directors.html).

2. A. J. Anderson, unpublished memoranda, Simmons College, Graduate School of Library and Information Science, Boston, 2002.

3. Murray Hiebert and Bruce Klatt, *Encyclopedia of Leadership: A Practical Guide to Popular Leadership Theories and Techniques* (New York: McGraw-Hill, 2001).

4. Robert M. Fulmer and Marshall Goldsmith, *Leadership Investment: How the World's Best Organizations Gain Strategic Advantage through Leadership Development* (New York: American Management Association, 2001).

5. William J. Rothwell and H. C. Kazanas, *Building In-house Leadership and Management Development Programs: Their Creation, Management, and Continuous Improvement* (Westport, Conn.: Quorum, 1999).

6. Robert D. Stueart and Barbara B. Moran, *Library and Information Center Management* (Littleton, Col.: Libraries Unlimited, 1998), 289.

7. Robert J. House and Ram N. Aditya, "The Social Scientific Study of Leadership: Quo Vadis?" *Journal of Management* 23 (May–June 1997): 409.

8. Allen J. Morrison, "Developing a Global Leadership Model," *Human Resource Management* 39 (summer–fall 2000): 117–31; Margaret E. Alldredge and Kevin J. Nilan, "3M's Leadership Competency Model: An Internally Developed Solution," *Human Resource Management* 39 (summer–fall 2000): 133–45.

9. Daniel Goleman, "Leadership That Gets Results," *Harvard Business Review* 78 (March 2000): 78–90.

10. F. Kramer, "CEO Briefing: On Management and Leadership," *Investor's Business Daily* (December 21, 1992), 4 (quoted in Herman L. Totten and Ronald L. Keys, "The Road to Success," *Library Trends* 43 [summer 1994]: 37).

11. Hap Klopp and Tracy B. Klopp, *The Adventure of Leadership: An Unorthodox Business Guide by the Man Who Conquered "The North Face"* (Stamford, Conn.: Longmeadow Press, 1991), 61 (quoted in Herman L. Totten and Ronald L. Keys, "The Road to Success," *Library Trends* 43 [summer 1994]: 38).

12. Esther Wachs, *Why the Best Man for the Job Is a Woman* (New York: HarperBusiness, 2000).

13. Robert Barner, "Five Steps to Leadership Competencies," *Training and Development* 54 (March 2000): 51. See also D. Ulrich, J. Zenger, and N. Smallwood, "Building Your Leadership Brand," *Leader to Leader* (winter 2000), 40–46.

14. Warren Blank, *The 108 Skills of Natural Born Leaders* (New York: American Management Association, 2001).

15. Rosie L. Albritton and Thomas W. Shaughnessy, eds., *Developing Leadership Skills: A Source Book for Librarians* (Englewood, Col.: Libraries Unlimited, 1990).

16. Jo Ellen Misakian, "The 12 Pieces of Leadership," *CSLA Journal* 24 (spring 2001): 15–16.
17. Mark D. Winston, ed., "Leadership in the Library and Information Science Professions: Theory and Practice," *Journal of Library Administration*™ 32, nos. 3 and 4 (2001): 1–186.
18. Becky Schreiber and John Shannon, "Developing Library Leaders for the Twenty-First Century," *Journal of Library Administration*™ 32, nos. 3 and 4 (2001): 43–53.
19. Camila A. Alire, "Diversity and Leadership: The Color of Leadership," *Journal of Library Administration*™ 32, nos. 3 and 4 (2001): 100.
20. Donald E. Riggs, "Editorial: Academic Library Leadership and the 'Life of the Mind,'" *College & Research Libraries* 62 (May 2001): 212–13.
21. Richard T. Sweeney, "Leadership in the Post-Hierarchical Library," *Library Trends* 43 (summer 1994): 62–94.
22. Mark D. Winston and Lisa Dunkley, "Leadership Competencies for Academic Librarians: The Importance of Development and Fund-raising," *College & Research Libraries* 63 (March 2002): 171–82. See also Susan K. Martin, "The Changing Role of the Library Director: Fund-raising and the Academic Library," *Journal of Academic Librarianship* 24 (January 1998): 3–10.
23. Terrence F. Mech and Gerard B. McCabe, eds., *Leadership and Academic Librarians* (Westport, Conn.: Greenwood Press, 1998).
24. Ruth J. Person and George C. Newman, "Selection of the University Librarian," *College & Research Libraries* 51 (July 1990): 357.
25. Joanne R. Euster, *The Academic Library Director: Management Activities and Effectiveness* (New York: Greenwood Press, 1987), 38.
26. Brooke E. Sheldon, *Leaders in Libraries: Styles and Strategies for Success* (Chicago: American Library Association, 1991).
27. Patrick M. O'Brien, "Quality Leadership for the Twenty-First Century," *Journal of Library Administration* 11 (1989): 29.
28. Ibid., 28, 30.
29. Herbert Goldhor, "The Head Librarian as Administrator of a Public Library," *Illinois Libraries* 71 (September 1989): 311.
30. Donald J. Sager, "Evolving Virtues: Library Administrative Skills," *Public Libraries* 40 (September–October 2001): 270.
31. Joey Rodger, "Leadership, Libraries, and Literacy Programs: A Report of [a] Focus Group" (Evanston, Ill.: Urban Libraries Council, 1999) (available: http://www.urbanlibraries.org/focus.PDF).
32. Laurence Corbus, "Key Attributes for Library Administration," *Public Libraries* 37 (November–December 1998): 355–56.
33. R. Alec Mackenzie, "The Management Process in 3-D," *Harvard Business Review* 47 (November–December 1969): 86.
34. Beverly P. Lynch and Kimberly Robbles Smith, "The Changing Nature of Work in Academic Libraries," *College & Research Libraries* 62 (September 2001): 407.
35. Ibid., 413. For discussions of the qualities expected of other positions in academic libraries, see, for instance, Penny M. Beile and Megan M. Adams, "Other Duties as Assigned: Emerging Trends in the Academic Library Job Market," *College & Research Libraries* 61 (July 2000): 336–47; David W.

Reser and Anita P. Schuneman, "The Academic Library Job Market: A Content Analysis Comparing Public and Technical Services," *College & Research Libraries* 53 (January 1992): 49–59; and Association of Research Libraries, Office of Leadership and Management Services, *Changing Roles of Library Professionals,* SPEC Kit 256 (Washington, D.C.: Association of Research Libraries, 2000). John N. Olsgaard presents those qualities that public librarians should possess; see John N. Olsgaard, "Educational Preparation for Public Library Administration: A Model for Cooperation," *Journal of Library Administration* 11, nos. 1 and 2 (1989): 35–51.

36. Dana C. Rooks, "Terms for Academic Library Directors," *Library Trends* 43 (summer 1994): 56.
37. Ruth J. Person and Sharon J. Rodgers, *Recruiting the Academic Library Director* (Chicago: American Library Association, Association of College and Research Libraries, 1991).
38. Goldhor, "The Head Librarian as Administrator of a Public Library," 312.
39. Sager, "Evolving Virtues," 270.
40. Darlene E. Weingand and Noel Ryan, "Managerial Competences and Skills: A Joint Study in the United States and Canada," *Journal of Library Administration* 6 (spring 1985): 26–27.
41. Peter Hernon, Ronald R. Powell, and Arthur P. Young, "University Library Directors in the Association of Research Libraries: The Next Generation: Part Two," *College & Research Libraries* 63 (January 2002): 86–87.
42. Euster, *The Academic Library Director.*
43. Goldhor, "The Head Librarian as Administrator of a Public Library," 307.
44. Ibid., 307–8, 312.
45. Ibid., 310.
46. Sager, "Evolving Virtues," 270.
47. Eileen McElrath, "Challenges That Academic Library Directors Are Experiencing as Perceived by Them and Their Supervisors," *College & Research Libraries* 63 (July 2002): 314–15.
48. MLA Leadership and Management Section Leadership Program, "Attributes of Library Leaders: Leadership Reconsidered: Developing a Strategic Agenda for Leadership in Health Sciences Libraries," paper presented at Medical Library Association Conference, Dallas, Texas, May 22, 2002.
49. Riggs, "The Crisis and Opportunities in Library Leadership," 5.
50. Robert K. Greenleaf, *The Servant as Leader* (Indianapolis, Ind.: Robert Greenleaf Center, 1970).
51. Sarah M. Pritchard, University of California, Santa Barbara, "Thoughts of Other Academic Library Directors," *Library Cultures Exploring Dimensions of Change: A Series of Lectures and Panels* (Ann Arbor, Mich.: University of Michigan, School of Information) (available: http://www.si.umich.edu/library-cultures/academic/directors.html).

3

QUALITIES FOR ASSOCIATION
OF RESEARCH LIBRARIES (ARL)
DIRECTORS

[B]efore we can lead others we should know ourselves well.[1]

For years, an ongoing question that historians and psychologists have asked is, "What qualities make for a good President of the United States?" Those qualities appear to center on "being stubborn and disagreeable," as well as being "more extroverted, open to experience, assertive, achievement striving, excitement seeking and more open to fantasy, aesthetics, feelings, actions, ideas, and values." Historically great presidents rated low on "straightforwardness, vulnerability and order."[2] Many of these qualities translate well into a successful leader within higher education. Being stubborn may be appropriate at times, but being disagreeable may be counterproductive; it may alienate people and make it difficult to achieve organizational goals.

Various studies have explored the leadership qualities that should be possessed by successful college and university presidents, provosts, and deans. For instance, John R. Wilcox, director of the Center for Professional Ethics at Manhattan College, and Susan L. Ebbs, associate vice-president and dean of student life at St. John's University, discuss presidents and note that "successful leadership in higher education requires the ability to use more than one organizational model to respond to different situations and multiple realities." Some of the qualities essential to presidents are collaboration, proper ethical and moral behavior, a solid understanding of the issues confronting higher education and of the culture of institutions of higher education, shared values (centered on the institution's mission), and "creation of an atmosphere of trust."[3] To this list, others have added vision (a realistic, credible, attractive future for an organization or institution); dedication to the life of the mind; consensus building; being energetic; "high-level administrative experience"; "respect for and understanding of the student community"; "ability to inspire confidence of students, faculty, staff," and others; "ability to identify and analyze problems; conceive appropriate solutions, achieve resolution, and persuasively communicate decisions"; "a record of scholarship"; "understanding of the critical role that technology plays in the institution's ability to pursue academic excellence"; "documented fundraising success"; "a commitment to diversity"; and the "highest personal integrity and character."[4]

Reflecting on the presidency, Clara M. Lovett, president emeritus of Northern Arizona University, emphasized that successful candidates must have political savvy. They must also be "articulate, photogenic, and skilled in the art of self-promotion:...sartorial correctness" and good public relations; after all, "the goal is to look like the...president from central casting."[5] Her cynical appraisal focuses on her perception of what it takes to be selected for the position. Some individuals associated with search firms disagreed with her and felt that prerequisite qualifications include "a combination of leadership skills and motivation," out-of-the-box thinking, no-nonsense management, and "communicating effectively with boards and working with alumni and legislatures."[6]

Our past research has focused on the qualities that directors of libraries that are members of the Association of Research Libraries (ARL) need to possess today and in the near future—the next decade.[7] This chapter extends that research through interviews with selected directors about those qualities and through commentaries that some directors offered as they assessed those qualities. Neither that research nor this book examines the actual selection process to which Lovett refers and how the list of qualities plays out during that process.

OUR PAST RESEARCH

Using triangulation, or multiple methods of data collection (content analysis, in-person and telephone interviewing, and the Delphi technique) relevant to the problem under investigation, we identified and refined a set of qualities that respondents—approximately one-fifth of the ARL university library directors—considered important for the present and next decades. Table 3.1 identifies the qualities that apply to both management and leadership. It is clear that the qualities expected of ARL directors are extensive and are gained from years of experiences and opportunities that arise within local institutions and more broadly (e.g., from different experiences within professional associations or in community service).

Table 3.1
Qualities Important for ARL Directors

Managerial Qualities

Managing
  Is committed to service
  Is results oriented
  Communicates effectively with staff
  Delegates authority
  Facilitates a productive work environment
  Is willing to make tough decisions
  Promotes professional growth in staff
  Manages fiscal resources/budgets
  Engages in fundraising and donor relations
  Nurtures the development of new programs and services/refines existing ones as
    needed
  Develops various sources of funds (grants, gifts, contracts, fee-based services)
  Is committed to staff diversity (and is culturally sensitive)
  Ensures that planned action is implemented and evaluated
  Facilitates the group process*
  Resolves conflicts*

Leading
  Builds a shared vision for the library
  Manages/shapes change
  Is able to function in a political environment
  Develops a campus visibility for the library
  Is an advocate for librarians' role in higher education
  Thinks "outside the box" (in new and creative ways applicable to the problem)
  Builds consensus in carrying out strategic directions
  Leads and participates in consortia and cooperative endeavors
  Is collaborative
  Is entrepreneurial
  Brings issues of broad importance to the university community, fostering wide
    discussion and action, when appropriate
  Demonstrates effective networking skills
  Keeps the library focused on its mission
  Changes/shapes the library's culture
  Develops and fosters partnerships with groups and organizations on/off campus
  Leads in a shared decision-making environment

Planning
  Sets priorities
  Plans for life cycles of information technologies and services
  Responds to needs of various constituencies
  Creates and implements systems that assess the library's value to its users
  Creates an environment that fosters accountability

Table 3.1
Qualities Important for ARL Directors (continued)

Personal Characteristics

Dealing with Others

Has credibility (trustworthiness, keeps commitments, and follows through)
Is evenhanded
Is self-confident
Is accessible
Treats people with dignity/respect
Is able to work effectively in groups
Is articulate (good oral/written/presentation skills)
Has a sense of perspective
Is diplomatic
Is open-minded
Is a good listener
Is able to compromise
Has a sense of humor
Has good interpersonal/people skills

Individual Traits (General)

Is committed to a set of values (integrity)
Is able to handle stress
Works on multiple tasks simultaneously
Is comfortable with ambiguity
Is committed to job and profession
Has self-awareness of strengths and weaknesses
Is honest
Is energetic
Is resilient
Is intelligent
Analyzes and solves problems
Has a variety of work experiences
Is able to "think on one's feet"—"wing it"
Is intuitive
Has broad knowledge of issues
Is able to ask the right questions
Manages time effectively

Individual Traits (Leadership)

Is focused on change
Exercises good judgment
Articulates direction for the library
Inspires trust
Is innovative
Has organizational agility
Is persuasive
Has reasonable risk-taking skills
Is optimistic
Understands that one does not have all the answers

Table 3.1
Qualities Important for ARL Directors (continued)

Personal Characteristics (continued)
Individual Traits (Leadership) (continued)
Is enthusiastic
Is an enabler and facilitator
Is committed to learning from mistakes
Takes initiative
Has team-building skills
Is committed to explaining decisions

General Areas of Knowledge
Scholarly communication
Understands the complex environment in which the library functions
Knowledge of financial management
Facilities planning (including remote storage and multi-use buildings)
Digital libraries
Planning (strategic, long term)
Trends in higher education
Information technology
Collection management and development (e.g., all formats, preservation, and acquisitions)
Outcomes (and accreditation) assessment
User expectations/information needs
Intellectual property rights
Management issues
Fundraising
Community's view of the library
Public relations
Service quality measurement*
Goals (educational, research, and service) of the parent institution*
Information delivery systems*
Publishing industry*
Resource sharing*
Information literacy*
Teaching and learning theory*

Note: The qualities within a category are ranked from most to least important for the next ten years. However, there was not unanimous agreement on the precise order of each quality.

*The mean score was less than eight on a ten-point scale, and subsequent rounds using the Delphi technique did not produce a higher ranking within the category. Thus, the quality has lesser importance.

Source: This table originally appeared in Peter Hernon, Ronald R. Powell, and Arthur P. Young, "University Library Directors in the Association of Research Libraries: The Next Generation," Part Two in *College & Research Libraries* volume 63, pages 85–87, January 2002.

SUPPLEMENTARY VIEWS

Thirteen directors, seven of whom participated in the original research, were asked to (1) participate in an interview that gauged their perspective on the importance of the qualities listed in Table 3.1, or (2) prepare written commentaries on the list of qualities. This section presents those results, thereby adding additional insights into the constellation of qualities relevant to ARL directors and those seeking the position.

The thirteen directors were selected in accordance with the procedures of our previous research, namely geographical representation, length of time spent as a director, and convenience for the investigators. We also relied on recommendations of some of the directors previously surveyed. The interviews were then conducted either in person or by telephone. In each case, the directors received a copy of the list of qualities (Table 3.1), as well as the interview questions, prior to the interview so that they could reflect on them.

Interviews

Eight directors participated in the interviews and considered the list (Table 3.1) as "very comprehensive" and reflective of these complex and ever-changing times in which university libraries currently find themselves or are likely to find themselves in the near future. When asked if the list applied to people of color, Director D replied that the qualities identified are "important to everyone. Leadership qualities are without color"; Director C concurred and thought that the list represented the items that "my provost uses to evaluate me."

Director H thought that, because the list was too long, it lost some of its impact on the reader. He endorsed the inclusion of chapter 6 of this book, which revisits the list, looks for commonalities, and refocuses the qualities. To guide a reconceptualization, he suggested grouping the qualities into four clusters: (1) "external role/policy formulation/citizen of the university/campus"; (2) "resource development, namely fundraising, research and development (i.e., grants), and generating new business opportunities (entrepreneurship)"; (3) "library culture, shaping the culture of the organization (i.e., influencing how people work in the organization)"; and (4) "strategic direction of the organization, which includes, for instance, planning, priority setting, and shaping 'where we are going.'"

The same director explained that resource development included all four areas identified. If his peers omit playing an entrepreneurial role as a key quality, in his opinion, they do not take advantage of the "total package" of opportunities. He emphasized that, under strategic direction, for example, he sets the vision for budget allocation, but he does not involve himself with managing the budget. If "I did, there would be little time to do other things—those that are my priorities."

Director A, who is currently going through a capital campaign, devotes 85 percent of his time to fundraising. He stressed the importance of entrepreneurship and explained that university administration and faculty may have dated notions of what libraries are. Entrepreneurship is a way to change perceptions and to ensure that the library plays an important role within the university. He also explained that technology has led to a change in the image of the profession as well as the nature of the work that librarians perform: "technology is central to the fabric of our work."

Director B downplayed the importance of fundraising and donor relations. She explained that this trait is important at some institutions but not at others. In some cases, the quality might be met through a development office and, in other instances, a library might not be part of the capital campaign.

Director C was surprised that the items listed under "general areas of knowledge" and marked with asterisks did not rate higher. In particular, he mentioned resource sharing and information literacy. He viewed the latter as "information literacy and information fluency" and explained that this quality enabled librarians to chart their course on campus as academic partners, not as subordinate players, in the educational process. Under "managing," he wanted to rename the quality on cultural diversity as "committed to, and having a record on, diversity."

Director D underscored the importance of directors having a "wide assortment of experiences," and she emphasized that "maturation is tied to experiences." Experiences that presented different challenges enabled her "to hone in on different qualities." Director B stated that "each of us has strengths and weaknesses as well as our interests—we pick our interests. Some of the qualities, however, relate to an individual's personality." According to her, over time, institutions have different expectations about those qualities they desire. At one time, they might want a "book person," another time someone with strengths related to technology, and even another time a "book person" again. Furthermore, some directors are not diplomatic and others are not good listeners. Also, having a sense of humor is helpful, but it is not essential. Clearly, the key to any list is realization of the issues and qualities that an institution regards as most critical at the actual moment it seeks a director.

Director D thought that the delegation of authority was important. Others in the organization, she explained, may have more expertise on some subjects. Further, as she pointed out, directors have so much to do that delegation is "key." She regarded herself as a generalist and would request a one- to two-page primer from a subordinate manager if she found a topic on which she was unfamiliar but needed information. As an example, she referred to metadata when it was beginning to generate extensive mention in the literature and in meetings. Other directors mentioned that the management of fiscal resources/budgets could be left to a budget officer, who might present the director with some choices for the expenditure of any remaining monies at the end of the fiscal year.

Director E referred to a shortage of librarians as "acute" in her organization (see chapter 1) and noted that she (and her middle managers) had to hire people from other disciplines and professions (e.g., accounting, law, and computer science) to handle some responsibilities, and they also had to reconceptualize some positions in order to attract a high-quality work force. At the same time, this library sought new hires who could fit into a changing and highly specialized organization. These individuals need to be externally focused. Further, with a number of retirements in the library over the past several years, people have been promoted more rapidly than "normal," and some of them lack the necessary training, set of experiences, and skill set. In this instance, the director believes that a shortage of qualified staff has resulted in a management and leadership crisis with which the library is trying to cope (see chapter 1).

Director A realized that an environment that aligns the library with the university could be difficult to create and maintain. For example, librarians who have been in the organization for years may be resistant to change because "they are being asked to do things they did not join the organization to do." For example, they might want to "catalog books and not work with faculty." He stressed the need to reeducate and retrain such staff members. While peer pressure may play a role in changing staff attitudes, the director needs patience and may have to wait for some of them to retire. At the same time, any newly hired librarian must fit into the type of change culture that matches the shared vision that the library is trying to implement. (His advice to students currently enrolled in a master's program in library and information studies is to develop themselves broadly so that they can fit into such a culture.) The competencies identified in Table 3.2 offer a good starting point. Moreover, gaining mastery of those attributes provides a solid foundation for achieving the qualities provided in Table 3.1 and for advancing to, and beyond, middle-management positions.

Director E did not see the next generation of directors as "pigeonholed"—having experience necessarily in only one type of library (e.g., only in university libraries); rather, there is cross-fertilization and increased opportunities for individuals to acquire qualities related to management and leadership in different settings and to transfer that knowledge, expertise, and experience to new settings. Increasingly, universities use search firms for senior positions. This enables them to identify individuals "a little outside the beaten path" who have relevant experiences to assume directorships. This type of individual tends not to be regarded as a "scholar/philosopher/thinker/writer," although he or she may engage in some of these activities on occasion. The "new breed" of director focuses on leadership and possesses many of the qualities identified in Table 3.1. Director E thought that professional development was important. Within this category, this director placed "retains currency in the profession of research librarianship through scholarship, instruction, and/or professional activities"; and "mentoring leadership development." Furthermore, she considered "recognition of others (having a reward structure)" as an important quality.

Table 3.2
Competencies for Research Librarians

Attributes of the successful research librarian include intellectual curiosity, flexibility, adaptability, persistence, and the ability to be enterprising. Research librarians possess excellent communication skills. They are committed to lifelong learning and personal career development.

1 The research librarian develops and manages effective services that meet user needs and support the research library's mission.
   Provides excellent service, customized to meet the needs of individual users
   Is knowledgeable about technology (theoretical and skills based) and applies it to improve services
   Anticipates user needs and critically evaluates and assesses existing and new services and systems to ensure that user needs are met
   Is innovative, seeking out and acting upon new opportunities and challenges
   Plans, prioritizes, and organizes work in order to focus on what is critical
   Participates in and applies strategic planning
   Is able to adapt business approaches to library operations to ensure accountability and the wise use of limited resources
   Communicates effectively with others outside of the library
2 The research librarian supports cooperation and collaboration to enhance service.
   Is able to work effectively with diverse groups, creating an environment of mutual respect
   Forms and maintains partnerships both within and outside of the university community
   Seeks opportunities to share expertise and knowledge
   Works effectively as part of a team
   Provides leadership
3 The research librarian understands the library within the context of higher education (its purpose and goals) and the needs of students, faculty, and researchers.
   Understands teaching, learning, and research, and seeks to provide services that will enhance these endeavors
   Is able to help users learn
   Is able to communicate the importance of library services to the higher education community
   Serves as an effective member of the university
   Is an expert consultant to the university on information
   Participates in and supports fundraising efforts on behalf of the university

Commenting on the number of directors who retire each year, Director E mentioned that the position can "wear people down" and that the "job is becoming too big for one person." This person commented on the volatile times resulting, in part, from globalization and information technologies,

Table 3.2
Competencies for Research Librarians (continued)

4 The research librarian knows the structure, organization, creation, management, dissemination, use, and preservation of information resources, new and existing, in all formats.
   Often has specialized subject knowledge to support collection development within the library and research and teaching within the university
   Understands how information and the research library support and enhance scholarly communication
   Understands the implications of information policy, including laws regarding copyright, licensing, and intellectual property
   Is able to evaluate critically and assess existing and new information resources in relation to user needs
   Describes and translates intellectual resources in a way that is useful to others
5 The research librarian demonstrates commitment to the values and principles of librarianship.
   Connects people to ideas
   Provides free and open access to information
   Demonstrates commitment to literacy and learning
   Shows respect for individuality and diversity
   Supports freedom for all people to form, hold, and express their own beliefs
   Preserves the human record
   Provides excellence in service
   Forms partnerships to advance these values

Research libraries are key partners in higher education, critical to the ability of universities to succeed in teaching and research. Research libraries will also continue to be important sources for the support and promotion of new developments in librarianship. Changes in the library environment, such as technological innovations and legal limitations on the use of information, will continue to offer opportunities for research librarians to gain and apply new knowledge. At the same time, the expertise that librarians have developed in organizing, providing access to, and preserving information will become more important than ever. The research librarian of the future will have more opportunities to support learning, enhance teaching, and improve research, providing services to the users of today as well as anticipating the needs of the users of tomorrow.

Source: Association of Southeastern Research Libraries, Education Committee, "Shaping the Future: ASERL's Competencies for Research Librarians" (2000), pp. 3–5 (http://www.aserl. org/statements/competencies/competencies.htm). Reprinted with permission from the Association of Southeastern Research Libraries, Inc.

and speculated that this volatility cannot continue forever. In the future, libraries, for instance, will be in a "better position to manage the cost of technology." However, for the next decade, the qualities identified in this chapter will dominate the scene. A director, she believed, must be persistent, aggressive, restless, flexible, able to view service outside the "nine to five" box, enjoy dealing with challenges, and see opportunities to position the library in a role central to where the university is moving—develop a strategy or vision and market it. The person is political in the sense that he or she "plays at an institutional level—helping the institution at all levels and on issues important to it." In doing so, the director "provides value to the institution beyond the area of the library" and competes for resources campuswide. The director also takes advantage of opportunities to "increase the value of the library to the university," to engage faculty and administrators in a dialogue about information seeking and use, and to participate in campuswide committees that do not deal directly with the library.

The directors interviewed reemphasized the distinction between management and leadership, and considered their role as more one of leadership than of management. Some of the key leadership qualities on the list relate to communication with others as well as building a shared vision for the library and being collaborative. The fundamental qualities, they said, will not likely change over time, especially since the library will remain "an integral part of the university community.... The library needs to find ways to work in the university environment to solve problems faced by the university at large."

Noting interconnections among the qualities, they thought that the list might be regrouped, with some items comprising a subgroup of more general qualities. For example, some of the "managing" qualities (e.g., commitment to service, able to make tough decisions, and effective communication with staff) are the direct result of implementing leadership. Director B thought that the resolution of conflicts was directly related to making tough decisions, and she was surprised that participants of the Delphi study (which directly resulted in creation of Table 3.1) did not rate conflict resolution higher.

The directors considered the "personal characteristics" important for future directors, as these characteristics focus on "how leaders of the organizations deal with people." Director A emphasized that, for the library to be integral to the university and the direction it is going, the staff must think differently (e.g., assume new roles and responsibilities) and share a common set of priorities. In such an environment, the director must lead and "take care to convince others so that a trust relationship emerges." The director must not penalize staff members if they make mistakes. Director D suggested that "individual traits (leadership)" might include integrity, which encompasses "consistency, fairness, and predictability." She would place integrity at the top of the list.

The directors did not see the personal characteristics as ones that individuals can necessarily acquire. Director A urged schools of library and information studies to develop a checklist for the evaluation of prospective students. Such a checklist could then be used to judge individuals on the extent to which they are good listeners, have a good sense of humor, are intelligent, are intuitive, are comfortable with ambiguity, are optimistic, and, most importantly, are aware of their strengths and weaknesses. Two other key qualities are "works on multiple tasks simultaneously" and "acquires effective team-building skills."

The directors considered the "general areas of knowledge" as important because these areas illustrate the broader context in which libraries find themselves. They noted that the director must have some knowledge of, and appreciation for, each of the qualities listed. However, the director need not master all of them. Director A considered public relations as a good example. It is critical, he asserts, that libraries engage in this activity and that directors delegate the responsibility. However, a director cannot be ignorant of the topic and what the library is trying to accomplish.

Director B considered the most important general leadership foci as scholarly communication, understanding the environment in which the library functions, digital libraries, planning, and trends in higher education. She thought that, over time, some of the qualities that did not rate highly (e.g., service-quality measurement) would become more important. She also saw areas such as collection management and development as ones that could be delegated. Regarding information technology, "you need to know about it, but that knowledge does not have to be deep."

Looking at the entire list (Table 3.1), Director F identified as most important those qualities related to administrative style, leadership, and "excellent administration." According to this person, more specifically, these qualities relate to: identifying which possibilities are feasible; contributing theoretical concepts and ideas; thinking in terms of systems and ensuring that other staff do the same; being an extrovert ("some administrators are introverts, but they are not as effective"); applying logical analysis to problems and making realistic assessments of facts; taking an active role in university affairs; being energetic; thinking in terms of long-range planning; being engaged in the operation of the organization (a direct management style); taking pleasure from management; appreciating challenges and questions (viewing questions as opportunities to "check on my own ideas"); moving quickly toward making a decision and being happy once that decision has been made ("some people prefer to receive ideas and are reluctant to make decisions")—"the danger is that a person may appear impatient and too anxious to reach a decision"; designing strategies so that the organization achieves its goals; being a good problem solver ("take charge quickly when problems arise"); being goal oriented; appreciating having good people around (i.e., a good management team); rewarding others for their contributions in reaching decisions and solving problems; being independent and results oriented; developing a good administrative structure for managing the organization; and taking pleasure in how people interact and provide value to the organization.

Director E concluded her interview by raising a question for the profession to consider, namely, "What do we do with your data? We should not ignore them." As a supporter of on-the-job training and leadership institutes, she thought that such efforts should focus on selected qualities—those that they could legitimately impart. Director G was also concerned about how the qualities could be achieved. In her view, directors needed to identify those individuals who appreciate challenges and who are likely to be the next generation of leaders, and to devote the time necessary to nurture them, as well as provide experiences from which to learn. "Regrettably, I see too little of this occurring today; my generation mentored the next one, but I do not see a number of present-day directors truly carrying forth the tradition."

Some of the other directors (e.g., Director D) partially disagreed. They explained that organizational structures have "become more specialized" and that associate/assistant/deputy directors (AULs) should be mentoring department heads. They suspected that AULs might resent directors bypassing them and directly mentoring those lower in the structure. Still, the perception is that mentoring does not occur to any significant extent.

Director G saw a potential leadership crisis looming (see chapter 1). "It is up to the whole profession, including library schools and professional associations, including the American Library Association and the Association of Research Libraries, to address this situation" and avert that crisis, thereby ensuring that libraries attract the talent necessary to lead libraries effectively as they encounter new challenges and opportunities. Yet, "neither the library schools nor the associations," in her opinion, "have shown much interest in the issue." She was also concerned that the pool of applicants and the group of present-day directors "is uneven in quality. There are some good leaders and some not so good ones." Like Director F, she did not see leadership as the exclusive domain of the director, and, as she emphasized, "we should not feel threatened by this." Libraries, she explained, should contain a number of leaders and a director should be willing to let this occur.

Commentaries

This section moves from the anonymous commentary of the interviewees to the responses of five seasoned, and named, library directors.

Rush Miller (Hillman University Librarian, University of Pittsburgh)

My goodness, when I read the list of attributes, I am amazed that any of us can possibly do all of this at once! Then, I remembered that most of it is not done by us at all, but by our very capable and underappreciated assistants, department heads, and development officers. One of the nice things about being in an average ARL library is that the resources arrayed to meet goals are so much greater than in other academic libraries.

I cannot pick out two or three of these things under "managerial qualities: managing" as being more important than the others. It seems to me that the list is pretty tight already. In some situations or environments, one of the

qualities might rise to the top. To be effective, a manager has to delegate successfully. But delegating implies trust, communication, nurturing, training,
and so forth. One has to be able to garner resources, both within the university and from fundraising and grants. That is essential to one's success. It is
no longer optional as an activity, or even as a skill. I cannot imagine how an
ARL director can be successful if he/she is not adept at fundraising and advocacy. The danger for us all is to become mired in the "management" aspects
of our jobs, the day-to-day activities, decisions, and problems. I find that
often the less I know about day-to-day stuff, the better I lead. I would want
to know if something is a major issue or problem, but would delegate the
handling of routine matters to others and let them manage.

Sure, we all have to make tough decisions. That is a cop-out. If we make
decisions sound tough, we exaggerate our importance as directors. Everyone
makes tough decisions. Some librarians, I can imagine, make a tough decision to stick with the organization and not desert it. Life is a tough decision
for some people. Our decisions are not nearly so difficult as that of our
provosts and presidents or even of our deans of arts and sciences. Those are
people with tough choices to make every day. Our decisions are less life-and-
death or earthshaking matters. I have never seen a library ruined totally by a
director, but I have seen universities ruined by presidents.

Resolving conflicts is an interesting one. Who in an organization really
resolves conflicts? I would suggest that, if a director is the person resolving
conflicts, he or she is too mired in day-to-day problems and issues. What is
the personnel office of the library for? What do department heads and assis-
tant/associate/deputy directors (AULs) do? In our library, I am *not* the "go-
to" person for resolving conflicts unless it is an appeal of a decision; then it
falls to me.

I also do not think communication is as important as we say it is. Sure it is
important. What is more important is to put in place a structure for communication and allow it to happen at all levels. Yes, we are committed to service,
along with everything else, including diversity, cultural awareness, and professional growth. This is like saying that motherhood is a good thing. My
question is, "What does it mean?" I do not know a director who is committed to poor-quality service or to discrimination.

A critical issue or attribute is not a commitment to these things, it is a
proactive and practical approach to making them happen. Is that the same
thing? Not to me.

I really do not know about "facilitating a productive work environment."
What is that? If it means structuring an organization for efficiency and effectiveness, I agree. If it means boosting the troops' morale all the time, I firmly
disagree.

I should say one more thing as an aside: I am tired of hearing directors talk
about staff morale as an issue. It is not an issue that we should waste time on.
Directors cannot motivate staff and create positive morale. In my view,

morale is something that is a person's own responsibility. I do not hold my provost or chancellor responsible for my morale, and I do not expect anyone in our libraries to hold me responsible for their morale. Morale is a complicated concept that relates more to a person's outlook and personality traits than to management. This morale-focused thinking leads to dishonest annual evaluations, designed not for honest feedback and correction but for positive reinforcement of even mediocre behavior to "motivate" the staff member. In fact, I see more damage done to libraries by directors and managers who try to motivate, instead of assess, than anything else, and it is usually related to misguided notions of morale. It is bad management.

Promoting professional growth is important, but it has to be done with the allocation of resources. So the primary attribute is that a person has the courage to allocate resources to accomplish positive behavior on the part of staff. In other words, if you want a staff to develop professionally, you have to put in place real incentives to reflect rewards for certain behaviors. If you want them to publish, you reward it in the merit system or promotion system. If you want them to go to an American Library Association (ALA) or some other kind of professional meeting, you pay their way and also give them credit for it tangibly. That is more important than encouraging the behavior through pep talks or speeches.

Turning now to "leading," I certainly find these qualities to be the absolutely critical ones for a director. The ones under "managing" are far less important and mostly should be carried out by others. Leading is where the buck stops for the director!

It is the responsibility of an ARL director to see the big picture of how the mission of the libraries fits into the mission of the university, even to see how the university serves a public good. That is vision, one of the past, the present, and the future. Vision focuses on the core values of our profession and how they can be made relevant to the present and future.

The most important quality, in my view, is that a director must be able to question time-honored assumptions. Almost no one else on the staff can do this, with the exception of AULs (but not always). Everyone else is mired in day-to-day activity and processes that are based on past activities and processes. They cannot see the forest for the trees most of the time. It is only the director, one hopes, who can think beyond the current environment, recognize trends and their impact, and manage people toward change. And change is key. We are living in an age of change. Because much of the change is not well thought-out or grounded, it produces poor results.

Campus visibility is something that a director does not do consciously, but it is a result of good leadership. If you build a solid library system that is forward-looking, you never have to worry about the image of the library on campus, or the support for it either.

Not all success is collaborative or consensual, and I would argue that we place too much emphasis on this in ARL libraries today. Generally our styles must be consultative, but I would never subsume the interests of my university or library to those of others for the sake of collaboration, unless there was an overriding public good that was indisputable. As a result, I do not agree that collaboration is vital.

I think entrepreneurship is probably a good thing, if by this we mean the ability to take advantage of opportunities and see them. If we mean developing fee-based services and such, I do not see that as a major issue.

Shared vision, shaping change, creativity, and changing the traditional culture of a library system have my votes as the most critical of these qualities. If I have had any success at the University of Pittsburgh it is from changing the culture—from feudalism to a republican form of government.

Regarding the qualities listed under "planning," it is essential to create a serious, strategic plan for a library system and then implement it over time, correcting it all along. Accountability is also a key issue for directors.

Under "dealing with others" and the "individual traits (general)," in the section on "personal characteristics," the most important qualities are having a set of values, comfort with ambiguity, and self-awareness of strengths/weaknesses so he or she can hire AULs who complement his or her honesty and intelligence. The rest of the qualities are just buzzwords. Under "individual traits (leadership)," judgment is a key one. Sound judgment leads to trust. Change focus, yes, I could have written that one, but it should not be overemphasized. Some stability is good too! To be good, one has to be persuasive, focused on ideas and not personalities, optimistic to a fault, and agile. These are more important.

The qualities listed under "general areas of knowledge" reflect the complexity of our environments today. You really do have to know a lot about many things, and such knowledge depends on the circumstance. My Ph.D. in Medieval History served me well when I came to Pitt and was faced with a feudal society. I could quickly grasp it and work within to change it. I recognized the culture, and I am not kidding about this.

Some of the qualities, such as real outcomes assessment, are wishful thinking. I would really like to see the person who has that figured out for an ARL library! I do not know anyone who has. You do not have to be expert at these issues, but you do have to appreciate and have familiarity with them. And, you have to know where to go for information about them. The organization itself needs this expertise, but does a director? It is impossible to know that much about all of these qualities. That is why we hire, train, and educate department heads and librarians. Do I have to be an expert in digital libraries, or should I be hiring experts to run my digital library? I need to know things at one level, and others perhaps should be expert at a more pragmatic level.

Finally, understanding the complexities of our environment is the most important base of knowledge. The rest are questionable to me. Clearly, the list of qualities presented in Table 3.1 is solid and gives us much on which to reflect.

Joan Giesecke (Dean of Libraries, University of Nebraska–Lincoln)

The complexity of the director's position in ARL libraries is reflected in the wide variety of attributes identified in Table 3.1. These qualities, including leadership competencies, are important in helping identify the skills and preparation needed by library leaders who aspire to the director's position.

While all of the qualities play a role in the director's job, the ones that I find most essential are self-confidence mixed with optimism and ability to build a shared vision. Self-confidence and optimism are keys to success. In today's uncertain and changing environment, directors make risky decisions while trying to guess about the future. Whether a library is adding or replacing an automated system, adding instructional technology, or changing services, the director needs the self-confidence to forge ahead despite the uncertainty of the technological environment in which libraries operate. Some decisions will prove to be successful guesses; others will not. Despite failures and mistakes, the director must keep the end objective in mind and move the library forward. Without confidence in one's self, it is difficult to face uncertainty and change continually, and move forward to bring the organization into the twenty-first century. Self-confidence also provides the incentive to act because then we believe we can make a difference. It provides us with the positive outlook, namely we need to believe we can solve problems. It also gives us the ability to enter potentially stressful situations with a sense that things can be made better. We can bounce back from failures and not give up when things go awry.

Without this positive approach, it becomes difficult to face change and turbulence continually in our environment. Furthermore, as in most director positions at large universities, the director is unlikely to receive a lot of direct feedback from the campus. Feedback on performance and library success is more likely to come through indirect means, from overheard comments, from messages to librarians and staff, from satisfied patrons, or from successful funding initiatives reflecting campus support. The director needs the self-confidence to appreciate indirect feedback as a measure of success.

Furthermore, optimism is a key part of successful self-confidence. Espousing a forward-thinking, optimistic approach to the challenges faced by today's libraries can bring more campus support than will a negative approach. Optimism is not a Pollyannaish, "head in the sand" view of the world. Rather, it is an ability to see the glass half-full—to see possibilities within challenges that will help move the organization forward even in poor times. Optimism keeps one focused on the future. When challenges such as a decrease in budgets, a poor economy, or a lack of administrative support occur, a director who is optimistic will find the opportunities buried in these challenges and will then convey these to the staff. A poor economy may be an incentive to assess workflow and increase efficiency. A lack of administrative support may be an incentive to design a marketing strategy to promote the library outside the institution and build support among the library's constituents. An optimist will see building an advocacy group to make the library's case to the administration and governing bodies as a positive option rather than as a necessity to offset a lack of supportive elements on campus. Without optimism and self-confidence, it is difficult to weather successfully the bad economic and political times and position the library to succeed when the environment improves.

The second key attribute that builds success is the ability to build a shared vision, one of the key elements of a learning organization. When the vision for the libraries is shared and understood among all staff, the result will be a sense of commitment by the group to a shared set of images of the future. Staff will also understand the principles, practices, and values by which the library hopes to achieve the shared vision. When the vision is shared and values are understood, staff will be better able to make decisions and design workflow that will help the organization achieve its vision in a coordinated manner. A small group within the library cannot develop the vision for the library in a vacuum. Today, the library's vision should come from conversations with the campus, the community the library serves, and all members of the library staff. Working with a broad coalition of library supporters, patrons, and staff, a successful director can lead processes that will result in a vision that meshes well with the community the library serves. A successful, tailored vision will resonate with constituents in ways that a generic internal vision will not. The director needs to be able to build a network on campus and within the libraries that will ensure appropriate input, development of a successful vision, and the acceptance and adoption of that vision by the community.

With a shared vision in place and self-confidence, a library director can design and work to implement programs and services that will meet the needs of the campus, the university community, and the broader library field.

Fred Heath (Dean and Director, Libraries, Texas A&M University)

Recently, my colleague who oversees academic and administrative computing at Texas A&M University, in the presence of our president and the chancellor of our system, characterized our two entities (computing and libraries) as "the two black holes of the University." His statement referred to our unremitting efforts to communicate to those responsible for resource allocation decisions on our campus and to our fellow deans, whose colleges generate the credit hours that fuel our enterprise and whose program support constitutes our only reason for being.

His tongue-in-cheek statement underscored the critical importance of advancing an understanding of the role that libraries and information technologies play in fostering learning and research in the major universities of North America. How is it that deans, provosts, and presidents come to embrace the notions that state-of-the art computing environments and top tier libraries, far from being "black holes" into which resources are poured to the detriment of faculty salaries, graduate stipends, and laboratories, are sine qua non for the success of the academic mission itself?

In times of scarce resources, a reality across most of higher education these days, library directors who are unwilling to enter the politicized environment of higher education and who are unable to convey a clear message of shared risks and mutual benefits—heard and embraced at the highest levels of the organization—are certain to fail. At the beginning of my tenure at Texas A&M University, one of my colleagues on the dean's council remarked that his college was ranked second among like programs in the United States, and "were it not for the library, it would be ranked number one." Among all the attributes of a successful director, the ability to communicate a message of shared purpose, of the library's role in advancing the critical academic missions of the university, is the most important. That colleague is now one of the strongest supporters of our library mission.

At least to some extent, leadership is contextual. "Bear" Bryant is a legendary icon in the football-crazed South. He exercised his genius at institutions, Texas A&M and Alabama, fully prepared to subscribe to the values and passion he brought to the game. Whatever one may think of the game of college football, it is worth noting that at both schools he revived dormant programs and developed a raised standard of expectation that is sustained to this day. It is also worth speculating that had fortune taken him to (unnamed) institutions where the game is less venerated, his football acumen might have gone unnoticed and unappreciated by the general public.

And, so it is with the business of research librarianship. The institutions that comprise ARL membership are the apex of the complex of North American colleges and universities that in their totality represent an intellectual asset that is the envy of the rest of the world. Yet, none of those universities are blessed with a surplus of discretionary resources ready to be dumped unbidden into the "black hole" of their research libraries. At every institution, central planners are able to project revenues from every likely source—endowment, appropriation, tuition, and contracts—and earmark all of those resources toward the components that comprise the academic mission.

So how does the director, caught up in what is essentially a zero-sum game, sustain and advance the library program in even the best of times? The answer is "with agility and entrepreneurship." The task at hand is, simply, to understand resource allocation processes on campus, and to devise stratagems that advance the shared academic mission without placing at risk the programs and priorities of colleagues who oversee other key university programs. At Texas A&M University, part of the answer was found in identifying statutory authority that permitted the assessment of fees for the enhancement of academic programs. With the support of the president, the provost, and the deans, and with the endorsement of student government organizations, the library has introduced new fees that direct almost $7 million annually into collection building. Likewise, the libraries have advanced their grant-seeking and private giving efforts, with the resulting success of securing grants from both the National Science Foundation and the Fund for the Improvement of Postsecondary Education of the U.S. Department of Education, while securing endowments to support professorships for seven of its most prestigious faculty.

Libraries succeed where they are perceived as being essential contributors to the intellectual process that defines the core being of a great university, an essential partner whose success does not come at the expense of others who share a similar commitment to the academic enterprise. Library directors succeed when they are able to deliver that message.

In every endeavor, change is always upon us. To continue the football analogy, Bear Bryant, an early convert to smash-mouth defense and ball control, when questioned about the value of the forward pass to college football, remarked that when a team threw the ball only three things could happen and two of them (interceptions and incompletions) were bad. He then proceeded to unleash, upon an unsuspecting Southeastern Conference (SEC), the strong arms of Joe Namath and Kenny Stabler, and via the forward pass dominated the football scene in the South for a decade. As schools adjusted, instituted their own wide-open offenses, and began to score more points and hold the ball for longer periods of time, he switched with equal alacrity to the clock-consuming, ball-control Wishbone offense, and made the SEC his playground for another ten years.

In an academic setting, libraries hold no monopoly upon the impact of change on their operations. The surging presence of information technology that has fundamentally altered information-seeking behavior among students and faculty alike has its counterparts across the university. Where faculty in another era might congregate at one location in order to exchange ideas and foster collaboration, they now work in real time with colleagues across the globe. Where libraries struggle with the rapacity of commercial publishers, whose stockholders demand optimal return on investment and whose monopolistic control of the marketplace allows pricing strategies unparalleled in almost any market sector, the colleges must contend with their own pressures. Those colleges also exist in an international marketplace, where the retention of established faculty whose talents are sought worldwide places enormous pressures upon budgets. The best young faculty seek those programs best able to offer them the start-up laboratories and other expensive facilities most likely to ensure their success in the new environment of the worldwide collaboratory.

Library directors who succeed are those who are agile in the face of unremitting change. Waving the bloody shirt of publisher exploitation may gain a modicum of sympathy for libraries among others in the academy, but it will not solve the underlying problem. Only by engaging the entire community, by changing the underlying fundamentals that drive market-based scholarly communication, will the academy succeed. Librarians must confront the necessity of continuing change, and view it not as a threat, but rather as an opportunity. With the right leadership in our libraries, the current threat to scholarly communication is not something for scholarship merely to endure; it is the departure point from which new paradigms will emerge that ensure scholarship will *prosper.*

In summary, let me acknowledge that I believe there are characteristics that define the successful attributes of leadership. Charley McClendon, former successful coach of the Louisiana State University Bengal Tigers football team, once said of Bear Bryant that he was the kind of football coach who could take his players and beat yours. And then he could take your own and beat his.

If there is a common theme to these eclectic thoughts, it is that libraries and librarians are part of something larger. Respect for colleagues and the multiple missions that define a university, and the ability to work effectively in a team environment, are traits evident in the library leaders I most admire. I guess I feel the single, most important characteristic of a leader is the ability to find the worth and respect the dignity of every individual. Bryant once said there were three kinds of ballplayers: those who were good and knew it; those who were good and did not know it; and those who were no good and did not know it. He had, he said, won more games with the last group than any other kind of football player. From that ability to discern, other things follow.

Miriam Drake (Professor Emeritus, Georgia Institute of Technology Library)

In looking at the attributes and qualities important to library directors it is clear that directors' positions need to be filled with deities and divine creatures. There are few, if any, earthlings possessing all the desired knowledge, skills, abilities, personality traits, and attributes. Each director has a unique combination of attributes, knowledge, intelligence, and managerial skills.

Most library directors spend their time in the midst of many muddles. The competing demands of various stakeholders and constituents tax the most intelligent, politically savvy, and charming of directors. Library budgets rarely are sufficient to provide all needed services, materials, equipment, facilities, and staff. Creating satisfaction for one group may result in revolt by another group. Senior administrators rarely understand why the director cannot create miracles, while the staff often has difficulty understanding the priorities and difficult trade-offs a director must make.

Different institutions need different processes, programs, and talents at different times. Four qualities help the director succeed: insight, adaptability, knowledge, and courage. Insight relies on observing, listening, discernment, intuition, and analysis. Insight uncovers "the way things are done around here," expectations, politics, and other elements essential to leadership and management. Misreading the environment or power structure or not understanding the cultures can lead to problems even if a director is bordering on the divine. Understanding the cultures will help the director use appropriate existing skills and develop new skills needed for success in the organization.

Within the library careful assessment of existing biases, talents, potential for leadership, and management is part of observation and listening processes. While position descriptions for ARL directors and public library directors have elements in common, the reality is that each library is unique and requires the appropriate blend of talents, skills, and attributes. Some library staff look for a visionary, some want a leader, some want a manager, and some want a fundraiser and person to deal with external matters while they are left alone to do as they wish. After some years of consistent leadership and direction new talents may come to the fore, culture may change, and staff may view the world differently than when the director arrived. The person at the top often sets the tone and the expectations despite teams, team leaders, and "flatter" organizations.

Search committees for library directors in academe usually consist of faculty members with good intentions and no idea how libraries work or what is needed to manage and lead a large organization. Many university presidents and provosts also are ignorant. They cannot figure out why libraries are so complex. Their goal often is to hire someone who will keep the faculty and students off their backs about the library. There are exceptional presidents, provosts, and city officials who understand and appreciate the library's contributions to the effectiveness of the university or municipality. They share the director's vision of what the library can be. They also value the intelligence and managerial talents directors bring to their positions.

Since earthling library directors cannot create the ideal environment in which they can do their best work, they must adapt to the institution, its cultures, and the talents of existing library staff. Directors must be willing to change and develop skills and knowledge needed for the job. Adapting to the management style of the institution is important. Ignoring the style, politics, processes, and power structures is dangerous. Directors need to adapt to changing environments, events, circumstances, and people both internally and externally. A change in university presidency, a new provost, or a new mayor can result in dramatic shifts in the power structure, financial rewards, budgets, and processes. When these changes occur, directors must call on their abilities to adapt and help library staff adapt to a new environment.

Knowledge is essential to the director's success. Staying ahead of the staff, management colleagues, top administrators, and others provides flexibility and ability to win friends for the library. Library directors need broad knowledge in many fields. They need to be voracious readers in a variety of areas and able to relate readings to their jobs. Library directors daily interact with people from a variety of backgrounds and occupations. They need to speak many languages including sports, finance, development, information technology, higher education, management, planning, and others. They need to relate to the contexts of individuals from many backgrounds.

In addition to insight, adaptability, and knowledge, a library director of an ARL library or public library needs courage to make decisions that may result in significant change or that are unpopular. Directors need to trust themselves and their intuition based on tacit knowledge and experience. Each person sees the world according to her/his context and how he/she models the world. Contexts and models are different. A cataloger is not going to model the world the same way as an information specialist who deals with customers all day. The richness and variety of models, contexts, and the ways different people work are essential to effective library operations. The director's context is the parent institution and the various views of important stakeholders, including, for instance, staff, customers, and top administrations. The director's model may be a vision or a carefully crafted strategic plan.

The courage to make decisions and take risks for the benefit of the parent institution is a personal matter. Courage is not a common characteristic among people in academe or political institutions. Most decisions made by directors are relatively low risk. Occasionally, a director will be confronted with a decision in which the consequences of a courageous decision are far more beneficial than the safer choice. The courage to take the risky road may or may not be rewarded in the short run. The director's insight into the institution and its culture will determine how courageous the director can be.

Sarah M. Pritchard (University Librarian, University of California, Santa Barbara)

It may be misleading to suggest that the qualities ideal for the director of an ARL library are somehow unique and distinct from those needed to be an effective director of a large college or public library. The management and leadership skills and abilities needed do not vary much, judging from my personal experience and professional interactions. Common to all are, for example, the crucial need to understand the environment of one's parent institution; to appreciate the impact of societal and technological trends on the nature of library users and services; to serve as an effective synthesizer and communicator of issues in two directions, from the inside to external constituencies, and vice versa; to have a structural understanding of one's organization and how to change the structure as needed to move ahead; to have courage and decisiveness; and to convey trust and credibility such that one can mobilize existing resources, develop new ones, and deliver the right services therewith.

Buried in Table 3.1 is a trait that may indicate that survey respondents were aware of this point; the individual trait "has a variety of work experiences" should mean more than just doing some work in cataloging and some in reference. It should mean that the director worked in various types of libraries in different parts of the country, maybe even spent time in the world of vendors, consortia, or foundations. We are too narrow in our expectations of the proper career path, and some search committees may unfairly stereotype director candidates who have not come up through the ranks. Yet, those may be the people best able to see the commonalities of the big picture, who have patience and perspective, can communicate with a variety of kinds of people, and come with access to new or different knowledge and collegial networks.

Context

Few traits on the list are limited to ARL directors, or even to directors per se. Many are traits that I hope associate directors and department heads display. What is different about ARL libraries is the research library mission and, specifically, the aspects of the mission that may not relate to any current constituencies: collecting of more unusual materials in all formats and languages; building of very comprehensive collections; collecting of unique primary sources that may not be used for a very long time; having a sense of responsibility for some portion of nationally important cultural heritage; piloting and developing digital initiatives; and needing to retain and preserve enormous amounts of material. All library directors must explain their mission in terms of the mission of the parent institution; but for a research library, even within research universities, the demand for assessment based on current outcomes is so strong that it may be a challenge to justify the expensive investment in a distant future. The director must have an acute awareness of the context of the research university, of the activities of peer institutions, and of the arguments that will ensure success by aligning goals with this broader context.

Understanding of the external environment entails a number of the skills and knowledge areas listed in the figure. It is not so much any one area that is important; again, it is the synthesis, the sense that these externalities as a whole are critical factors in shaping the way the library will operate. The library director may not need detailed knowledge of the publishing industry, copyright law, demographics, public finance, and advanced digital and network technologies, but he or she will indeed need to know the basic outlines and latest twists of each, and that all of these and more are factors shaping the way the library will work. Higher education itself is the central context, and the director has to make the connection between education trends and ways of doing business and the necessary changes in information services.

In glib conversation, I have claimed that all library directors should simply study anthropology. We know that every organization has a culture; and more than that, every organization, including higher education, municipal government, and private corporations, operates according to formal and informal mechanisms of power, ritual, kinship, and barter. One does not have to like any given culture, but one had better understand it in the observational sense or be doomed to a short or dismal tenure. While many who are both participants and observers of organizations decry the politics and games

that go on within, these are simply more structures to be learned and used in a positive way.

The degree of complexity, the number of external variables, and the rapidity of change are such that the director is constantly working in a state of ambiguity, multiple foci, and incomplete information. Many other abilities (especially good intuition, a sense of strategies and alternatives, and an understanding of calculated risk) then come into play. Most lower-level staff hate this ambiguity and juggling so it is also up to the leader to find ways to reassure them. A lot of this simply comes from personal credibility and perseverance, since underneath almost everyone realizes that there is no certainty in most of our institutions. In the midst of ambiguity, while calculating those risks and taking steps with a strategy in mind, the director draws on a contradictory combination of patience and insistence on getting things done.

Communication and Outreach

All directors need to be largely handling external relations, even if "external" means simply the rest of the campus. This is not always appreciated by staff, who may feel neglected and as if the director does not know what is going on at home. It is a matter of being able to communicate effectively to them the ultimate benefit of those external relations, and the fact that the library exists to serve a series of external constituencies. These include the faculty and students, other campus departments, the community, perhaps the state legislature or a board of regents, library and higher education consortia, vendors, publishers, foundations, donors, alumni, parents, and the media. Writing and speaking to each of these groups may require shifts in tone and vocabulary, even using quite different arguments when addressing the same issue. Keeping the message consistent across this plethora of audiences can be tricky, but is essential to credibility internally and externally.

Communication for the director is as a filter and interpreter linking the internal and the external. The need to translate between what seems like two sides of the same family cannot be taken for granted. Inside the library, frontline staff may be too quick to impose some rule arbitrarily for internal workflow reasons; the director needs to ensure that at every level, it is not just a question of customer service but of really understanding why we are all here. This is easier than the other direction. In the university, for example, some other administrator may say, "but we weren't talking about the library," when the topic was the first-year [undergraduate] experience, or the need to provide better server backups for faculty research data, or the upcoming weekend power shutdown that supposedly will not affect anyone because classes are not in session and administrative offices are closed. The director sometimes risks being thought of as self-centered, always claiming the library is related to whatever is being talked about; the director needs to have the ability to show the more general case, the relevance of information services,

the role of librarians and not just of libraries, the potential to advance academic programs and community initiatives. Most satisfying is communicating with those outside the university like donors, community agencies, journalists, or others who may be skeptical, disconnected from the university, or deluged by requests, and seeing them light up when you are able to synthesize and explicate the exciting dynamic of the contemporary research library.

Management

The director needs to draw on a structural and systemic view of the library and the university. It may seem contradictory, but this seems to imply both an organic and an analytical model, the ability to see the parts and the whole and the mechanisms that link them. The central management skill is the allocation of all types of resources (people, dollars, space, and materials) in a constantly shifting environment, following some strategy that is envisioned as resulting in the services valued by the parent institution. So the important areas of knowledge are an understanding of the structures of personnel, finances, collection development, technology, and space planning—not in their micro details, but in their broad policies and goals and with a view towards holistic outcomes. In budgetary matters for example, it is sometimes thought by those not used to administration that the question is how big a budget has the person managed. In my experience the more important question (and one generalizable across varied organizations) is how complicated a budget has one managed. It matters less whether it is $3 million or $30 million, but into how many categories those dollars have to be equitably sub-allocated, and how many types of funds one must track (current, endowed, one-time, allowed to be carried over or not, self-generated revenues, restrictions on use, and the like). The ways in which resources can be shifted rapidly and creatively to respond to unforeseen pressures and opportunities are different from institution to institution, and the director needs to learn the particularities quickly, even overruling hidebound internal staff methods of dividing the pie.

Personnel issues are central. While the director is not, and should not be, involved in much frontline supervision, it is he or she who sets the tone for the whole organization in terms of equity, empowerment, staff development, openness, inclusivity, and accountability. The need for staff to perceive the director as available to them cannot be underestimated; the actual amounts of time may be small except when there is some crisis, but the director who is remote and uncommunicative will have a much harder time generating the sense of commitment and communication at lower levels that will ensure a productive department. Personnel matters, unfortunately, can cause the most nasty and personal attacks and can drag on for years. Most large research libraries have their own internal human resources office, but I have found that cultivating campuswide support from human resources, equal employ-

ment opportunity, ombudspersons, union stewards, and general counsels is also highly beneficial. In many universities, the library can be a leader in innovative personnel practices because of its relatively large staff size and long hours; libraries have led the way in such programs as flexible and compressed schedules, diversity initiatives, staff development, group dynamics, and safety and ergonomics planning. The director is key to promoting visibility on campus of librarians and library technical/clerical staff as employees who have much to contribute to the general university community.

The degree to which a director must focus on internal management fluctuates with different phases in the life of the organization. Often a new director will inherit a series of festering problems that require hands-on attention; however, the goal is eventually to empower the staff and facilitate communication such that the library's routine daily services run themselves. To achieve this sense of a well-running operation, good middle managers are fundamental, so the skills of delegating and coaching and metatraining are important. The number of direct reports in a library of 60 or a library of 300 may be the same—three to six is common, a little more if you include administrative assistants, development officers, and others beside librarians. The relationship and guidance between a director and his or her management team speak volumes; we can all point to directors of long tenure who have successfully cultivated, and sent on to promotion, a series of associate directors. The evolution over the course of being an AUL, from focusing strictly on internal management to gaining and utilizing the external and context-rich perspective outlined above, is a key aspect of making this transition and becoming a viable candidate for a directorship.

Gestalt

Being a library director takes a certain amount of courage, a trait that has not surfaced during this research project. Many things that happen are not fun or pleasant, and difficult decisions must be made without always having the support of staff or of other campus administrators. On library programmatic or budgetary matters, one may have to make a case in front of audiences who do not have a clue as to what is really involved in delivering information services or why they should care, and who view the library director as a competitor for scarce resources. Usually when it comes down to it, even with a management team, one feels personally responsible for every facet of library progress and it can be a rather lonely feeling. After years of teamwork, you are in a job where there is only one of you in the organization and one on campus and you are accountable; perhaps it is no surprise we like to go to director-only professional meetings. Turning this around to the positive, it is typical that a good library director will exhibit a distinctive individuality, a unique leadership and communication style that results from the combination of vision and strategy and thinking out two or three steps ahead. There is not just one way to exhibit this individuality, as evidenced by the many different director personalities; perhaps that is why we are driven to try to understand the underlying component traits.

Directors and high-level administrators need metaknowledge—more than just the specific skill or topic, it is the ability to put those pieces together, to choose when to use which management style, to know when to delegate or not to do so, when to work through formal university committees versus informal backroom deals, to know which are the subjects in which you must absorb yourself personally and which are better handled by hiring expert staff or consultants. There is some overlap and repetitiveness on the lists of traits as now itemized; while initially the classificatory tendency may be to be a category "splitter," the more effective trait for leadership and broad communication is to be a "lumper," to show the commonalities and to know how to use a great many individual skills and knowledge areas in concert.

Every trait and area of knowledge on this list is useful, valuable, and evident in our colleagues. Is it too much to expect to find them all? We agonize about the challenges and the difficulties and wonder how we will ever grow the next generation of leaders; we have to tell them how much fun it is when it all comes together.

CONCLUSION

As time goes on, qualities currently considered of lesser importance may become more prized. It may be that future generations will value more someone who is inquisitive, has good coaching skills, and demonstrates imagination. It is critical that the present and future generations of those aspiring to directorships understand the qualities valued in the organization they are joining and will be leading.

As the directors interviewed emphasized, there will be variation among institutions regarding those qualities most prized in a director. Those qualities, most likely, center on the perceived issues most critical to the institution at the time of the search. Over time, the qualities needed may shift. Still, those interviewed thought that the list serves a useful purpose—it offers guidance to institutions seeking directors and to those individuals interested in pursuing directorships. Most likely, the directors and AULs, together, possess the widest array of qualities; the directors interviewed realize that AULs complement them.

Chapter 6 takes the qualities discussed in this chapter and the two subsequent chapters and regroups them. The purpose is to identify interconnections among the items, thereby increasing the value of the list to future generations of aspiring directors, as well as researchers and groups trying to deliver programs aimed at addressing a set of qualities effectively and efficiently. At any rate, all of the directors interviewed are campus leaders and view leadership qualities as essential for the present and next generation of university library directors.

The research library of today and tomorrow is a dynamic, service-oriented organization, supporting a diverse clientele with a wide range of sophisticated information, learning, and teaching needs.[8]

NOTES

1. University at Buffalo, State University of New York, Leadership Development Center, "Resources—Tips and Tricks" (Buffalo, N.Y.: Leadership Development Center, July 24, 2001 (available: http://www.leadership. buffalo.edu/tips1.shtml).
2. "APA News Release: What Makes a Good President?" Washington, D.C.: American Psychological Association, August 2000 (available: http:// www.apa.org/releases/presidents.html).
3. John R. Wilcox and Susan L. Ebbs, *The Leadership Compass: Values and Ethics in Higher Education,* ASHE-ERIC Higher Education Report, no. 1 (Washington, D.C.: George Washington University, School of Education and Human Development, 1992), 41.
4. The University of Alabama at Birmingham, Presidential Search Advisory Committee, "Attributes of Leadership," n.d. (available: http://www.uasystem. ua.edu/Administrati...Search/attributes%20of%20leadership.htm).
5. Clara M. Lovett, "The Dumbing Down of College Presidents," *The Chronicle of Higher Education* (April 5, 2002), B2. For a dated but still relevant discussion of the selection process see Ruth J. Person and George C. Newman, "Selection of the University Librarian," *College & Research Libraries* 51 (July 1990): 346–59.
6. "Letters to the Editor," *The Chronicle of Higher Education* (May 10, 2002), n.p.
7. Peter Hernon, Ronald R. Powell, and Arthur P. Young, "University Library Directors in the Association of Research Libraries: The Next Generation: Part One," *College & Research Libraries* 62 (March 2001): 116–45; Peter Hernon, Ronald R. Powell, and Arthur P. Young, "University Library Directors in the Association of Research Libraries: The Next Generation: Part Two," *College & Research Libraries* 63 (January 2002): 73–90.
8. Association of Southeastern Research Libraries, Education Committee, "Shaping the Future: ASERL's Competencies for Research Librarians" (2000), 3 (available: http://www.aserl.org/statements/competencies/competencies. htm).

4

QUALITIES FOR ASSOCIATION OF COLLEGE AND RESEARCH LIBRARIES (ACRL) LIBRARY DIRECTORS

> Leaders who connect well with people are ahead of the game. Everything else can be acquired through education, experience, or professional development.[1]

In the preceding chapter, the leadership attributes of Association of Research Libraries (ARL) library directors, which had been compiled from position advertisements and refined through a Delphi protocol administered to a group of sitting directors, were enlarged upon by several additional directors who furnished more extensive commentary. This chapter, which covers mid-sized libraries tracked by the Association of College and Research Libraries (ACRL), adopted the same research strategy. Through an analysis of leadership traits within the same library sectors and through a comparison with other types of libraries, it may become possible to refine the profile of desired traits and to suggest approaches for acquiring core competencies needed for future library leadership. This challenge will be addressed in subsequent chapters.

DELPHI STUDY

Determination of the desirable leadership traits of smaller academic libraries began with a random selection of libraries compiled in an annual statistical compendium issued by the Association of College and Research Libraries, a division of the American Library Association.[2] Twenty libraries from this report were selected at random, with due regard for an appropriate mix of public and private institutions, and with consideration for institutions representing various sizes of institutions. All libraries were affiliated with four-year institutions, and no library selected held fewer than 100,000 volumes. Directors then responded to three successive rounds of e-mail designed to identify and refine leadership attributes.

Round One

The twenty library directors were asked to serve on the panel of experts for the Delphi component of this study. Each director on the panel received via e-mail a list of fifty-four unranked attributes compiled from the job advertisements listed in recent issues of *College & Research Libraries News* (see Table 4.1). Only light semantic editing was done to the raw list. The list was arranged under three major categories: managerial attributes, personal attributes, and areas of knowledge.

Each participant was asked to examine all of the attributes, and to respond with the following possible actions to refine the list: (1) to propose additional attributes; (2) to eliminate attributes that they believed were either inappropriate or duplicative; and (3) to recommend the repositioning of attributes which they thought might be placed under a different heading. Approval of the entire list as transmitted was also an option.

The directors deleted six attributes from the list. These attributes were (1) "institutional leader"; (2) "planning, implementing, and assessing strategic goals"; (3) "work collaboratively within library and campus and among consortium colleagues" (4) "demonstrated excellence in teaching"; (5) "experience with issues"; and (6) "experience with data archiving."

Nearly double the number of deleted items was considered important to add to the list. Attributes added to the list were (1) "ability to plan, implement, and assess strategic goals"; (2) "ability to work in collegial, networked environment"; (3) "excellent oral and written communication"; (4) "experience developing digital libraries"; (5) "a second advanced degree"; (6) "respect for scholarship and learning"; (7) "listening skills"; (8) "integrity"; (9) "flexible"; (10) "ability to work collaboratively with campus colleagues"; and (11) "commitment to quality services and resources." There were also a few relocations of attributes within the three broad categories.

Rounds Two and Three

Round two involved the ranking of attributes within the three categories. To make judgments on the various unranked attributes, participants were given a scale of one to ten, with one denoting "not important" and ten designated as "very important for the present and near future." Directors were asked to assign numerical values as an indication of the attribute's importance, and not its relative value to other attributes.

Only one item was deleted from the list during round two, "experience with facility planning and design." Somewhat surprisingly, there were no

Table 4.1
Academic Library Director Qualities for the Present and the Future (Preliminary Unranked List)

Managerial Attributes

Supervisory experience
Senior administrative experience
Proven facilitative leadership skills
Experience in positions of increasing responsibility
A record of innovative and effective leadership
Institutional leader
Demonstrated ability to identify trends
Understanding of and commitment to institutional mission
Documented record of supporting diversity
Firm commitment to quality
Proven ability to foster team building and participatory management
Planning, implementing, and assessing strategic goals
Vision in formulating programs and implementing strategies to integrate print and
    electronic resources

Personal Attributes

Have MLS (perhaps another degree)
Documented record of problem solving
Creative
Dynamic
Enthusiasm for work in an educational environment
Demonstrated ability to exercise mature judgment
Sense of humor
Excellent oral and written communication skills
Is service oriented
Articulate vision for library within the institution
High energy level

attributes added or removed in round three. Mean values were calculated for each of the areas: managerial attributes—8.21; personal attributes—8.72; and areas of knowledge—7.23. These aggregate mean scores for the three categories suggest that personal attributes are considered more important than the other two categories, an important outcome considered later in this volume. Attributes in only two of the areas, managerial attributes and personal attributes, received a mean score of 9 or higher. These attributes are listed in descending rank order below:

- Integrity;
- Strong interpersonal skills;
- Ability to serve as an advocate for the library;
- Excellent oral and written communication skills;

Table 4.1
Academic Library Director Qualities for the Present and the Future (Preliminary Unranked List) (continued)

Areas of Knowledge

Proven managerial ability with personnel and with fiscal, budgetary, and program matters

Experience with grant writing

Expertise in fundraising

Expertise with distance education

Demonstrated knowledge of library operations

Knowledge of an experience with change management

Experience with program assessment and evaluation

Demonstrated experience with automated library systems

Demonstrated experience as a senior information technology leader

Record of scholarly achievement

Knowledge of collection development

Experience with current technology and information systems as they apply to libraries

Work collaboratively within library and campus and among consortium colleagues

Serve as advocate for library internally and externally

Proven fundraising capabilities and success in securing funding support

Commitment to professional development of library personnel

Able to engage in facilities planning

Experience with collaborative arrangements between/among multicampus and statewide settings and other institutions

Demonstrated excellence in teaching

Strong interpersonal skills

Engage in long-range planning

Experience in planning or coordinating new library building projects

Experience managing or planning digital libraries

Experience with issues

Experience with information literacy

Experience with data archiving

Experience with facility planning and design

Experience with public relations

Experience with marketing of services and resources

Experience with scholarly communication

- Ability to work collaboratively with campus colleagues;
- Ability to articulate vision for library within the institution;
- Demonstrated ability to exercise mature judgment; and
- Supervisory experience.

Conversely, the three lowest-ranked attributes in each category were, in descending order:

- Managerial attributes: "commitment to diversity," "demonstrated ability to identify trends," and "experience developing digital libraries";
- Personal attributes: "high energy level," "dynamic," and "second advanced degree"; and
- Areas of knowledge: "experience with grant writing," "experience in planning or coordinating new library building projects," and "expertise with distance education."

Table 4.2 provides the final ranked list.

SUPPLEMENTARY VIEWS

Following the pattern in the chapter on ARL directors, a smaller group of directors who did not participate in the initial ranking exercises was asked to comment on the ranked list and to provide responses to some important supplementary questions about the attribute list and related issues. Four directors provided responses to the ranked list (see Table 4.2). The directors who responded to this request for more extensive commentary were: Elaine Didier, dean, Oakland University Library; David Gleim, dean of the Auraria Library, a midsized academic library serving 34,000 students and faculty of the University of Colorado at Denver, the Metropolitan State College of Denver, and the Community College of Denver; Lorraine J. Haricombe, dean of libraries, Bowling Green State University; and Mary Reichel, university librarian and Carol Grotnes Belk Distinguished Professor, Appalachian State University. Collectively, these library directors serve at geographically dispersed institutions with student populations and curricula of the mid- and larger-sized ACRL academic libraries. Verbatim questions asked of the directors are followed by their responses, all rendered as either exact quotes or very lightly edited remarks.

Is the Delphi ranked list of desirable attributes comprehensive/complete? Which ones are most important? Do you want to add/delete anything?

All respondents found the list comprehensive, but several preferred a slightly revised array of attributes.

Didier: The top six managerial attributes should be proven managerial ability in personnel, fiscal, budgetary, and program matters; ability to plan, implement, and assess strategic goals; proven facilitative leadership skills; proven ability to foster team building and participatory management; firm commitment to quality; and experience in positions of increasing responsibility. Under personal attributes, items one through seven remain in the same ranking, followed by flexible, listening skills, strong service orientation, sense of humor, high energy level, and dynamic. The top five knowledge attributes are knowledge of library operations, experience with change management, experience with current technology and information systems as they apply to

Table 4.2
Academic Library Director Qualities for the Present and the Future (Final Ranked List; Average Scores)

Managerial Attributes

9.0 Supervisory experience
8.9 Proven managerial ability in personnel, fiscal, budgetary, and program matters
8.7 Ability to plan, implement, and assess strategic goals
8.7 Ability to work in collegial, networked environment
8.7 Understanding of and commitment to institutional mission
8.6 Proven facilitative leadership skills
8.5 Proven ability to foster team building and participatory management
8.5 A record of innovative and effective leadership
8.5 Firm commitment to quality
7.8 Vision in formulating programs and implementing strategies to integrate print and electronic resources
7.7 Experience in positions of increasing responsibility
7.5 Commitment to diversity
7.2 Demonstrated ability to identify trends
6.6 Experience developing digital libraries

Personal Attributes

9.8 Integrity
9.5 Strong interpersonal skills
9.5 Ability to serve as an advocate for library
9.5 Excellent oral and written communication skills
9.3 Ability to work collaboratively with campus colleagues
9.1 Ability to articulate vision for library within the institution
9.1 Demonstrated ability to exercise mature judgment
9.0 Have MLS
9.0 Flexible
9.0 Listening skills
9.0 Commitment to professional development of library personnel
8.9 Respect for scholarship and learning
8.5 Strong service orientation
8.5 Enthusiasm for work in an educational environment
8.4 Sense of humor
8.3 Documented record of problem solving
8.0 Creative
7.9 High energy level
7.5 Dynamic
6.6 Second advanced degree

Table 4.2
Academic Library Director Qualities for the Present and the Future (Final Ranked List; Average Scores) (continued)

Areas of Knowledge

8.9	Knowledge of library operations
8.2	Experience with change management
8.1	Experience with current technology and information systems as they apply to libraries
7.9	Experience with program assessment and evaluation
7.8	Experience with information technology
7.5	Experience with long-range planning
7.5	Experience with collaborative arrangements between/among multicampus and statewide settings and other institutions
7.3	Experience with scholarly communication
7.3	Experience with public relations
7.2	Knowledge of collection development
7.2	Experience with marketing of services and resources
7.2	Record of scholarly achievement
7.1	Experience with facilities planning
7.0	Proven fundraising capabilities and success in securing funding support
6.9	Experience with information literacy
6.9	Knowledge of bibliographic control
6.7	Experience managing or planning digital libraries
6.4	Experience with grant writing
6.3	Experience in planning or coordinating new library building projects
5.1	Expertise with distance education

libraries, experience with long-range planning, and experience with public relations.

Gleim: In general, the list is pretty comprehensive. Clearly, the new director has to show up the first day on the job with a big toolkit of relevant experiences and skills. A vision, of course, is essential, as is the ability to make good decisions quickly with incomplete information. I also find I have to work hard to keep current with the trends and problems of higher education in general.

Haricombe: I think the list is comprehensive. I would like to add the dimension of gender. Many library directors/deans are women, but they face different challenges in higher education, where the field is still predominantly male. Women often walk a tightrope between being leaders and collaborators, firm and gentle, public and private.

Reichel: I want to start out with this point. Librarians (and staff) can be leaders at all levels of job responsibilities, and, in fact, a measure of success for an academic library director is how many leaders there are among his/her colleagues. While supervisory experience is important, I would put "proven managerial ability" first. When I see "experience developing digital libraries,"

I wonder why experience with teaching or cataloging or other activities is not listed. Under personal attributes, strong interpersonal skills are essential and I would list them right where they are; however, the overall phrase needs to be expanded to include the idea of working with different groups, students, faculty, staff, administrators, alumni, and donors. I would move listening skills higher. I love the inclusion of a sense of humor, and I would add a sense of perspective about one's own importance. Under areas of knowledge, I would move experience with grant writing higher.

Once the current directors of large and medium-sized academic libraries retire, where is the next generation coming from?

Are they coming exclusively from large and medium-sized academic libraries? Are they in associate/deputy/assistant positions? Is one of these positions more likely to lead to directorships?

Didier: They should/will come not only from large and medium-sized libraries. There can be very effective directors of smaller libraries where they learn the breadth of the role by wearing many hats.

Gleim: In my experience—and I have worked in two medium-sized and two ARL academic libraries in the past thirty years—the AULs [associate/assistant/deputy librarians] have been about the same age as the directors, that is, mid- to late-fifties. Really too old to have had much of a lengthy and meaningful career as a director.

Haricombe: The traditional path has been that the associate/deputy positions move up to the director/dean levels. We will probably see this trend continue—search committees are tough and will usually look for administrative and scholarly credentials.

Reichel: Academic libraries will need a new generation of directors during this year, in five years, and in ten years. Directors who start five and ten years from now are really the next generation. Future directors are not exclusively in assistant administrative slots (the associate/assistant directors are the directors of next year). Future directors are now line librarians or department heads/coordinators.

Must they have a record showing progressive administrative responsibilities related to an academic library?

Didier: Yes, but it might not be in an academic library.

Haricombe: I, too, would strongly advocate for administrative experience; however, I think we often overlook leaders at other levels of the organization (e.g., department chairs, coordinators, and branch librarians). We should not sit back and wait for leaders to emerge; we have a responsibility to mentor, nurture, and cultivate emerging leaders on the job and through professional development opportunities.

Reichel: My own career path included twenty years of experience in both ARL and non-ARL libraries before becoming a director. I graduated with my master's in 1972. I suspect for my generation of librarians that men became directors with five or fewer years of experience. The generation before us saw men becoming directors two, five, seven years out of their library education. Barbara Moran's research on career paths would give more information than my own gut sense.[3]

Any preferred length of time for gaining experience at the upper level of academic library administration?

Didier: Minimum three to five years, and preferably more. One year is not enough for the breadth of experience necessary.

Haricombe: To experience the broad array of administrative duties, I would advocate for three to five years. Notwithstanding the length of time there will be a learning curve coupled with experientially based learning and adjustment to the organization and campus cultures.

Reichel: In regard to a preferred length of time for gaining experience, I do not think that length of time is the key factor. Factors which I think are more important include significant budget and personnel experience, as well as exposure to fundraising. Many of the library issues that directors deal with are explored and understood in different positions, but effective handling needs to be based on enough experience to know what is possible and how to maximize budgets. While supervisory experience is valuable, it is also necessary for directors to understand a range of personnel issues and systems, both for librarians and support staff.

Is national standing in the profession required?

Didier: No, but it is very helpful.

Haricombe: A requirement of national standing in the profession may be appropriate in certain library types. I would be open to evidence of other professional involvement and impact at the local, regional, and state levels. Requiring national standing may limit an already shrinking pool even further.

Reichel: National standing in the profession is extremely helpful. My experience nationally has given me a pool of contacts whom I can call for advice and information, especially with difficult issues not suitable to explore on one's own campus. Directors can be successful if they have excellent campus standing and standing beyond the campus, in the state, regionally, or nationally. I do not think directors can serve as role models for their colleagues or have the breadth of understanding necessary if they are only involved on their campuses.

What, if any, is relevant nonacademic library experience?

Didier: Service in a large public library or as director of information or instructional technology or media services in an academic institution. The key is the breadth and complexity of the positions held and the number of personnel led and/or supervised.

Haricombe: Experience in information technology systems would be an asset. Experience in leadership positions at nonprofit organizations, experience in development work, and marketing skills are all relevant to library leadership roles.

Reichel: Relevant nonacademic library experience could include a range of possibilities, such as college teaching, university or college planning responsibilities, or other administrative positions. That kind of experience does not substitute for the master's in library and information science.

Any degree expectations? Leadership institutes?

Didier: Ph.D. preferred (for credibility with other deans and senior directors, and for more in-depth knowledge and experience gained from graduate studies beyond the MLS). Leadership institutes—yes, can be valuable both for knowledge gained and for the professional network developed in the process. The UCLA program seems to have fostered as much of the latter as the former. Also useful would be institutes with attendees from the broad spectrum of higher education.

Gleim: Both internally and externally, for about 75 percent of the communication and writing I do, plus the meetings I attend, any good senior administrator with general experience in higher education could effectively handle it. And the doctoral degree adds status. It is that other 25 percent that is the rub. Without lengthy experience and education in the state library profession and at least some standing in the profession on a state or national level, a director is not going to be taken seriously as a leader by colleagues in the library. And even with the help of solid AULs [associate/assistant/deputy librarians], a nonlibrarian director is bound to make some disastrous decisions, given the pressure and lack of information that directors work under.

Haricombe: At least a Ph.D., or an MLS and a Ph.D. in another subject.

Reichel: Earning a Ph.D. is very helpful experience as well as bringing a credential similar to other deans and directors. I would hope that more academic library directors would have the doctorate. Holding that degree raises the level of respect for the director and for the librarians as well.

Do you expect any changes in the knowledge and skills that will be necessary for the future?

Didier: Communication and interpersonal skills will become increasingly important: the ability to advocate for the library, develop marketing and outreach programs, develop partnerships with corporations and community groups, and conduct fundraising programs.

Gleim: Not so much a change in knowledge and skills as a change in emphasis. The newest librarians and staff I work with appear to be less "self-contained" than those when I began the profession in the early 1970s. By that I mean they seem to bring to their work a far greater set of expectations for others to meet than I ever did. Many of the faculty and staff I have directed in the past decade look to the senior library administration for self-affirmation, career guidance, moral support, and personal and professional development. At the same time, they bring with them the same healthy suspicion of administration that I had as a spear carrier in the profession. This is a strange mixture for a director to deal with. If the trend continues, future directors will have to be wizards in human resources as well as in walking the tightrope between being a friend and colleague of the faculty and staff as well as their leader.

Haricombe: Increasingly, libraries are getting involved with assessment of services, collections, facilities, instruction, etc. This was not the case in recent history. The recent LibQUAL+ surveys are generating new interest among librarians in statistical and data analysis skills to help interpret the needs, trends, and future directions for libraries. Corollary to this is the need for continuous review and planning. Increasingly, deans are expected to identify and cultivate donors and to collaborate closely with the development office. Healthy time management is also important. In my experience, I have found that heavy demands are made on personal time. Deans are expected to be more visible around campus; library staff make demands on the dean's time; and there are visitors to the library, social events, etc. Libraries offer public relations opportunities between the university and the community to build those bridges. Understand administration's view of the library. Know the stakeholders and involve them in library activities. Communicate often and openly to the campus community. Create opportunities for the campus community to be proud of the library.

Reichel: The biggest change that I see is the need to focus on faculty, staff, and students as the users of library collections and services and to be attuned to their present and future information needs. Academic library directors cannot afford to be internally focused and weighed down with operational decisions. Keeping informed about campus issues as well as individual research pursuits and educational programs is essential. The same general stance is crucial for fundraising, which will become increasingly important in the director's position. Both state and private institutions need directors who inspire with their vision and who can raise additional monies to help the vision come to life.

What is your perception of the existing pool of candidates for the directorship? Do they tend to have the desirable traits?

Didier: The pool is limited due to personal circumstances such as being unwilling or unable to relocate due to family responsibilities or a spouse unable to relocate. The pool is also limited by the fact that many individuals are unwilling to work as hard or as many hours as most directors do, or they are not willing to take on full responsibility.

Gleim: In general, the new library directors I am familiar with seem to be quite competent. But I really have not had much experience with evaluating recent candidates.

Do provosts/presidents have the same or different expectations for the successful candidate?

Didier: Their primary interest seems to be on chemistry/compatibility with themselves (or the ability to control them) rather than on particular knowledge of the field or leadership ability. They also tend to see the position as specific to the library rather than having potential for broader campuswide leadership.

Gleim: Presidents expect library directors to raise lots of money and to give them [the presidents] lots of opportunity to take credit for new library labs, new electronic resources, building renovations, substantial gifts and grants, and so on (and to keep out of the newspapers). And this is as it should be in academe. On the other hand, the provosts I have worked with spend 90 percent of their time solving problems caused by mistakes made by their deans and directors. Sex, money, and faculty troubles are the Big Three. Provosts expect library directors (1) certainly not to generate problems themselves with the Big Three and (2) to solve Big Three problems caused by others without involving the provosts. There is another expectation: to turn in all reports, memos, and strategic plans on time.

Haricombe: Provosts and presidents expect strong leadership in library deans/directors. We support the most important constituent groups at the university: faculty and students. Despite the decrease in library funding, the library still represents the university's investment in education and scholarship. My campus invested heavily in technological infrastructure for the campus community. The expectation is that university operations will increasingly move in the direction of automated services and electronic documents. Deans and their faculties are expected to show strong leadership in incorporating technology in the classroom and in other support services such as the library.

Reichel: Provosts and presidents also want directors who can provide and articulate vision and goals. Certainly they want directors who will follow personnel procedures and avoid costly staff appeals or lawsuits. In addition, provosts/presidents want administrators who will work well with other administrators at the same level. There is an existing pool of candidates with these capabilities, but it is the responsibility of every sitting director to promote the development of colleagues, both for local and national positions.

In your opinion, why would someone want to become director of a large or medium-sized academic library?

Didier: The opportunity to exercise leadership and to make a difference in the quality of library and information resources and services on a campus. The opportunity to be part of a campuswide leadership team and to think and function beyond the library.

Gleim: Only one reason: because it is fun. It is fun to see the changes one has brought about actually taking place and working successfully. "My god!

We have talked about networked, touch-screen printing for three years, and I finally found the money to install it and it really works and the kids love it." Unless directors can have fun every day with small victories like this one, then the overwhelming responsibility will burn them out in short order.

Haricombe: Different things motivate people to pursue goals. For me, it became a personal goal to aim higher after my first job as an administrator of a small college library. Unlike the academy, libraries have experienced consistent and rapid changes that offer new and different opportunities for future directions. The changes and challenges force us to employ creative imaginings to help define new directions for the library. I find that exciting. There is never a dull moment.

Reichel: There can be great satisfaction in making a difference in the quality and level of library collections and services; in helping students become better educated and information literate; and in supporting faculty research. Preserving our intellectual and cultural heritage is another strong motivator. Why would someone not want to become a director?

CONCLUSION

Library directors participating in the Delphi study generated a list of fifty-four attributes in the three categories of managerial attributes, personal attributes, and areas of knowledge. Highly ranked managerial attributes focused on communication skills, setting the strategic agenda, and collegiality. Low-ranked attributes included diversity, needs identification, and experience with developing digital libraries. Under personal attributes, integrity was the clear winner, followed closely by interpersonal skills and communication competencies. Bringing up the caboose were creativity, energy level, and possession of a second advanced degree. Top-ranked areas of knowledge included familiarity with technology, library operations, and planning/evaluation. Conversely, low scores were accorded to information literacy, bibliographic control, grant writing, building projects, and distance education.

It is important to remember that various attributes within the three categories were closely ranked with each other and often separated by not more than several tenths of a point. And it should also be pointed out that respondents were not asked to rate the primacy of the three major areas. Such an analysis may shed some light on the nature/nurture dimension of leadership development, that is, are leaders born or do they at least possess certain personal traits, or can various leadership skills be learned and successfully applied? Also, a fixed set of leadership attributes would certainly not apply in every situation, and the local employment context must be considered to ensure a good match for the particular skill set brought by the individual.

Comparing the rankings provided by the directors in this study with a list of attributes identified by long-term library leadership consultants Becky Schreiber and John Shannon is illuminating. They identify six critical leadership traits: self-awareness, embracing change, customer focus, stands to take in the future, collaborative spirit, and bias for courageous action. Leaving room for slightly different phrasing but semantic similarity, there are two variables mentioned by Schreiber and Shannon which are not readily apparent in the listings in this study. The notions of self-awareness and a commitment to substantive change are not as starkly represented in the list of director-furnished traits in our listing. Self-awareness, in fact, may be particularly important, and it is a capacity that can be refined through various training and evaluative experiences.[4]

> If management practice is ever to be simplified into one unifying principle, I believe it will be found in self-reliance. [5]

NOTES

1. Lorraine J. Haricombe, dean of libraries, Bowling Green State University, interview with authors discussing comments on ACRL Delphi attributes, September 16, 2002.
2. Association of College and Research Libraries, *1999 Academic Library Trends and Statistics for Carnegie Classification: Doctoral-Granting Institutions, Master's Colleges and Universities, Baccalaureate Colleges,* compiled by Center for Survey Research [Thomas M. Guterbock, director, University of Virginia; Hugh A. Thompson, project coordinator, ACRL] (Chicago: Association of College and Research Libraries, 2000).
3. See Barbara B. Moran, "Career Patterns of Academic Library Administrators," *College & Research Libraries* 44 (September 1983): 334–44.
4. Becky Schreiber and John Shannon, "Developing Library Leaders for the Twenty-First Century," *Journal of Library Administration* 32 (2001): 35–57.
5. Margaret J. Wheatley, *Leadership and the New Science* (San Francisco: Berrett-Koehler, 1994), 147.

5

———•◦•———

QUALITIES FOR PUBLIC LIBRARY DIRECTORS

> Libraries, like other public organizations, require effective leadership in order to provide quality service.[1]

Academic librarians are not the only ones worried about the adequacy of the pool of future directors and interested in the desirable attributes of library directors. While the topics have not received as much attention in the professional literature as they have for academic library directors, public librarians are also concerned about these issues. According to Laurence Corbus, "In the search for a library director, nearly every public library board seeks several key attributes. While these attributes vary,...nearly every public library board of trustees seeks the elusive W.O.W., a director who Walks on Water."[2] Consequently, the authors decided to ascertain optimal attributes for public library directors, and, as is reported in chapter 6, to compare attributes of public and academic library directors.

DELPHI STUDY

In order to facilitate a comparison of the desirable attributes of public library directors with those of directors of libraries belonging to the Association of College and Research Libraries (ACRL) and the Association of Research Libraries (ARL), a decision was made to limit this part of the study to attributes of directors of large and medium-sized public libraries. After consulting with several library and information studies educators, directors of the American Library Association's (ALA) Office for Research and the Public Library Association (PLA), and the professional literature, we, somewhat arbitrarily, decided that a public library must serve a community of at least

25,000 people in order to be considered a medium-sized library and to qualify for the study. No upper limit was set for medium-sized libraries, as large
public libraries were to be included in the study as well. (ALA's Office for
Research has operationally defined medium-sized public libraries as those
serving a population of 25,000 to 99,999 and large public libraries as those
serving populations over 100,000.)

As was the case with the consideration of attributes for directors of libraries
belonging to ACRL and ARL, the purpose of this phase of the study was to
identify desirable attributes and to achieve a consensus on the most important ones. In order to accomplish this objective, the Delphi technique (see
chapter 4) was once again employed as the primary method. The twelve
members of PLA's Small and Medium-Sized Libraries Committee and the
thirteen members of its Metropolitan Libraries Committee were contacted
by e-mail and asked to serve on the panel of experts for the Delphi study. It
was assumed that libraries belonging to the latter group would qualify as
large public libraries; directors of libraries belonging to the former group
were asked not to participate if their libraries served populations of less than
25,000. (One exception was made for a director with thirty years of management experience in slightly smaller public libraries.)

Round One

For round one of the Delphi study, eligible directors were e-mailed an
unranked list of attributes of possible importance to present and future directors of large and medium-sized public libraries (see Table 5.1). The attributes
were identified through a content analysis of job ads in *American Libraries*
for the past five years as well as an examination of the professional literature.
(Please note that the Appendix to chapter 2 complements the list nicely.) The
attributes were organized into three categories: managerial attributes, personal attributes, and areas of knowledge.

The participants were asked to first examine the list of attributes, by category. They were then to take any of the following actions that they thought
would improve the list: (1) add additional attributes to any group; (2) cross
off any attributes that they thought were not important enough to be in
such a list or that duplicated other listed attributes; and (3) move any attributes that they believed better belonged under a different heading by cross-
ing off the attributes and writing them under the preferred headings. In the
unlikely event that they thought the list was fine as provided, they were to so
indicate.

Eleven panel members responded to the mailing for round one. A few of
the directors did recommend moving a few attributes to different categories.
Some suggested changes in the wording for certain attributes. All of them
crossed off some attributes and/or added new ones. If a change suggested by
a participant seemed to represent a consensus of the group (at least several of
the participants suggested the same change), then the list was modified
accordingly. Consequently, two attributes were moved from the managerial

Table 5.1
Attributes for Round One

Managerial Attributes

Appreciates the vital role that the library plays in the community
Advocates for the library with community and governmental agencies
Able to engage in effective problem solving
Able to manage all facets of library operations
Is an innovative leader
Able to integrate technology into the library
A proven fiscal manager
Has demonstrated ability in marketing/public relations
Has strong leadership skills
Has good team-building skills
Has good staff management skills
Able to engage in outreach services
Able to engage in grant writing
Able to motivate/inspire staff
Has willingness to engage in community service
Has willingness to further the professional development of staff
Has an aptitude for fundraising
Able to engage in facilities management
Able to work effectively with staff
Able to work effectively with community/civic organizations

Personal Attributes

Has a vision of the vital role of the public library and can articulate it
Has good collaborative skills
Projects a professional manner
Is comfortable with diverse populations
Has a sense of humor
Demonstrates excellent oral and written communication skills
Demonstrates excellent interpersonal/people skills
Exhibits a strong commitment to public service
Has an appropriate number of years of professional experience
Has progressive administrative/managerial/supervisory experience
Has progressive programmatic experience
Is politically savvy
Is a creative problem solver
Has integrity
Has master's degree in library and information science

Areas of Knowledge

Technological innovation
Current library practices
Emerging trends
Budgeting
Long-term planning
Experience in working effectively with library boards
Experience in working effectively with friends' groups
Experience in working effectively with state/local public officials
Collection development
Spanish language

category to the personal category, and four were moved from the personal category to the managerial one.

Eleven attributes were deleted from the list. They were: (1) is an innovative leader; (2) is a proven fiscal manager, (3) has strong leadership skills, (4) has good staff-management skills, (5) is able to engage in grant writing, (6) has an aptitude for fundraising, (7) is able to engage in facilities management, (8) has a sense of humor, (9) is politically savvy, (10) is a creative problem solver, and (11) has knowledge of emerging trends.

On the other hand, seventeen attributes were added to the list. They were: (1) able to develop a bond/levy campaign, (2) able to work with a union, (3) able to develop long-range plans in collaboration with community, (4) willingness to encourage board and other community members to be advocates, (5) willingness to further own professional development, (6) demonstrates innovative leadership, (7) is active professionally, (8) knowledge of library public services, (9) knowledge of library technical services, (10) knowledge of intellectual freedom, (11) knowledge of community analysis techniques, (12) knowledge of building and remodeling, (13) knowledge of law and public policy issues relevant to the public library, (14) knowledge of personnel administration, (15) knowledge of measurement and evaluation methods, (16) knowledge of project management, and (17) knowledge of current human resources administration.

Round Two

The revised list of attributes resulting from round one of the Delphi study was mailed to the participating directors. The attributes were again listed within categories in no particular order. The participants were asked to assign a value of one through ten to each attribute, thereby indicating its importance to directors for the present and next ten years. One was to mean "no importance," five to represent "moderate importance," and ten was to designate "maximum importance"; but the participants were told that they were to feel free to assign any value to the ten-point scale. They were allowed to assign the same value to more than one attribute. The assigned value was to represent the attribute's importance to a director, not its value relative to the other attributes. In other words, the directors were to assign values independently. Twelve directors participated in round two, but two responses were received too late to include in the analysis. A mean value was calculated for each attribute in the list used for round two.

Total mean values for the three categories were calculated as well and were as follows: managerial attributes—7.73, personal attributes—8.21, and areas of knowledge—7.15. These statistics may tentatively suggest that the participating directors considered personal attributes relatively more important than the other types.

Round Three

Based on the values/importance assigned to the attributes in the second round, for round three the attributes were ranked by mean scores within groups; the higher the value, the more importance they attached to an attribute. For the third round, the participants were asked to check the list to determine if they wished to change the relative positions of any attributes within groups. To help the participants make such decisions, the attributes were broken down by quartile within groups (see Table 5.2). (Some quartiles had unequal numbers of attributes because of ties or rounding.) The directors were told that they could change the ranking of an attribute by drawing a line from it to the position to which they wished to move it, or by drawing a line through the attribute and writing it into the preferred space.

Eight directors completed the third round. Three of the participants recommended no changes in the list of attributes; one recommended one change; four recommended changes ranging in number from three to thirteen. However, several directors recommended one change, and so only that change was made in the list of attributes. "Able to communicate effectively with staff" was moved from the seventh position in the category of managerial attributes to the second position. With that one change, the researchers were satisfied that a consensus on desirable attributes for directors of large and medium-sized public libraries had been reached among the participants, and no further changes were deemed necessary.

Managerial attributes receiving a mean score of 9.0 or higher were

- Able to work effectively with library boards;
- Able to work effectively with staff;
- Advocates for the library with community/civic and governmental agencies/organizations; and
- Able to articulate/communicate the vital role of the library to the community.

Only one personal attribute—has integrity—received a mean score of at least 9 even though that grouping received the highest mean value. No area of knowledge received a score of 9.0 or higher.

SUPPLEMENTARY VIEWS

As was done in conjunction with the examinations of attributes for directors of ARL libraries and other academic libraries, a small number of appropriate directors were asked to comment on the final list of attributes. In this case, directors of six large and medium-sized public libraries were sent the final list of attributes ranked from most to least important within each category (see Table 5.3) and were asked to answer several questions about the attributes and related matters.

Table 5.2
Attributes for Round Three

Managerial Attributes

First Quartile
Able to work effectively with library boards 9.9
Able to work effectively with staff 9.3
Advocates for the library with community/civic and governmental agencies/
    organizations 9.2
Able to articulate/communicate the vital role of the library to the community 9.0
Able to engage in effective problem solving 8.9
Able to work effectively with community/civic organizations 8.9
Able to communicate effectively with staff 8.9

Second Quartile
Able to work effectively with friends' groups 8.6
Able to work effectively with state and local public officials 8.6
Has willingness to involve staff in planning and development of services 8.5
Able to develop long-range plans in collaboration with library's community 8.4
Has good team-building skills 8.3
Has willingness to further the professional development of staff 8.1
Has willingness to encourage board and other community members to be
    advocates 8.1

Third Quartile
Able to work effectively with a union 7.5
Advocates for the library with individual constituents 7.3
Able to work effectively with the general public 7.3
Has good time-management skills 7.1
Has good understanding of job assignments and workflow 6.9
Appreciates importance of marketing/public relations 6.8

Fourth Quartile
Able to manage all facets of library operations 6.5
Has progressive administrative/managerial/supervisory experience 6.5
Able to integrate technology into the library 6.2
Has a good sense of when to pitch in 6.1
Has an appropriate number of years of professional experience 6.0
Able to design outreach services 4.1

Personal Attributes

First Quartile
Has integrity 9.5
Has a vision of the vital role that the library plays in the community 8.8
Demonstrates effective oral and written communication skills 8.6
Demonstrates excellent interpersonal/people skills 8.6

Table 5.2
Attributes for Round Three (continued)

Personal Attributes (continued)

Second Quartile

Exhibits a strong commitment to public service 8.5

Is comfortable with diverse populations 8.4

Has good collaborative skills 8.3

Able to motivate/inspire staff 8.3

Has good organization skills 8.3

Third Quartile

Projects a professional manner 8.1

Able to demonstrate innovative leadership 7.9

Has willingness to further own professional development 7.5

Fourth Quartile

Is active professionally 7.3

Has willingness to engage in community service 6.8

Areas of Knowledge

First Quartile

Trends and innovations in libraries 8.7

Current library practices 8.4

Long-term planning 8.4

Budgeting and financial planning 8.1

Intellectual freedom 8.1

Law and public policy issues relevant to public libraries 7.9

Second Quartile

Demographic changes in the community 7.8

Economic changes in the community 7.8

Functions of library boards 7.7

Roles of state/local public officials 7.5

Business administration 7.3

Third Quartile

Functions of friends' groups 7.1

Knowledge of the general public 7.1

Community analysis 7.1

Emerging technological trends 6.9

Building and remodeling 6.8

Concepts of collection development 6.7

Project management 6.7

Current human resources administration/personnel administration 6.7

Fourth Quartile

Measurement and evaluation methods 6.4

Library public services 5.9

Library technical services 5.7

Trends and innovations in education 5.5

Major foreign language(s) of community 5.2

Table 5.3
Attributes for the Supplementary Views

Managerial Attributes

Able to work effectively with library boards
Able to communicate effectively with staff
Able to work effectively with staff
Advocates for the library with community/civic and governmental agencies/
   organizations
Able to articulate/communicate the vital role of the library to the community
Able to engage in effective problem solving
Able to work effectively with community/civic organizations
Able to work effectively with friends' groups
Able to work effectively with state and local public officials
Has willingness to involve staff in planning and development of services
Able to develop long-range plans in collaboration with library's community
Has good team-building skills
Has willingness to further the professional development of staff
Has willingness to encourage board and other community members to be advocates
Able to work effectively with a union
Advocates for the library with individual constituents
Able to work effectively with the general public
Has good time-management skills
Has good understanding of job assignments and workflow
Appreciates importance of marketing/public relations
Able to manage all facets of library operations
Has progressive administrative/managerial/supervisory experience
Able to integrate technology into the library
Has a good sense of when to pitch in
Has an appropriate number of years of professional experience
Able to design outreach services

Personal Attributes

Has integrity
Has a vision of the vital role that the library plays in the community
Demonstrates effective oral and written communication skills
Demonstrates excellent interpersonal/people skills
Exhibits a strong commitment to public service
Is comfortable with diverse populations
Has good collaborative skills
Able to motivate/inspire staff
Has good organization skills
Projects a professional manner
Able to demonstrate innovative leadership
Has willingness to further own professional development
Is active professionally
Has willingness to engage in community service

Table 5.3
Attributes for the Supplementary Views (continued)

Areas of Knowledge

Trends and innovations in libraries
Current library practices
Long-term planning
Budgeting and financial planning
Intellectual freedom
Law and public policy issues relevant to public libraries
Demographic changes in the community
Economic changes in the community
Functions of library boards
Roles of state/local public officials
Business administration
Functions of friends' groups
Knowledge of the general public
Community analysis
Emerging technological trends
Building and remodeling
Concepts of collection development
Project management
Current human resources administration/personnel administration
Measurement and evaluation methods
Library public services
Library technical services
Trends and innovations in education
Major foreign language(s) of community

The following directors provided responses: Josie Parker, director, Ann Arbor (Michigan) District Library; Robert Raz, director, Grand Rapids (Michigan) Public Library; Nancy Skowronski, director, Detroit Public Library; and Douglas Zyskowski, director, Southfield (Michigan) Public Library. These four public libraries serve a large city (Detroit), a medium-sized city (Grand Rapids), one of the largest suburban communities in the state of Michigan (Southfield), and a town with a major university and large high-tech industry (Ann Arbor). The questions asked of the directors and their individual, mostly verbatim answers follow:

Once the current directors of large and medium-sized public libraries retire, where is the next generation coming from? Exclusively from large and medium-sized public libraries? Are they in associate/deputy/assistant positions? Is one of these positions more likely to lead to directorships?

Parker: I believe the next generation will come from within the library profession, but they need to be recognized and groomed for the positions.

That is what happened to me, and I am much better for it. Future directors will more likely have had other professional experience prior to library careers or in addition to library careers.

Raz: Associate, deputy, and assistant directors do have a decided advantage.

Skowronski: Not necessarily just from public libraries. Academic middle managers have a lot in common with middle managers in large to medium-sized public libraries. I have to say that a deputy at a large urban library would have an edge over other middle managers.

Zyskowski: For the most part the next generation of library directors will, I feel, be coming from large or medium-sized public libraries. There will be, of course, exceptions where a director from a small library is able to "break into the ranks" of a medium-sized library. They will, in general, have held responsible positions either as associates, as deputies, or as assistant directors in their current jobs. Also, directors will move up from one size of library into a larger-sized library. I tend to feel that a deputy position is more likely to move up into the position of director of an organization.

Must they have a record showing progressive administrative responsibilities related to a public library?

Parker: I do not think it is necessary that directors have progressive public library administrative experience, only that they have had experience leading in a complex organizational environment.

Raz: Not necessarily related to a public library. The person who has demonstrated a progression through the ranks will have an advantage.

Skowronski: While they must have a record showing progressive administrative experience, it need not be limited to public libraries.

Zyskowski: Quite definitely they must have a record showing progressive administrative responsibility related to public libraries. This would be quite necessary.

Is there any preferred length of time for gaining experience at an upper level of public library administration?

Parker: (Had already noted that administrative experience in a public library was not necessary.)

Raz: Five years or three years plus other type of management experience.

Skowronski: Five to seven years.

Zyskowski: In general, the more time gaining experience the better. A minimum of five years working in upper level administration would seem to be an appropriate requirement.

Is national standing in the profession required?

Parker: National standing in the profession would be added value, but not an expectation.

Raz: No, only perhaps in a very large public library looking for the "prestige" factor.

Skowronski: Encouraged certainly, but not required. Professional involvement must be documented—whether it is local, regional, or statewide.

Zyskowski: In my mind, national standing in the profession should not be a requirement. That implies abilities and inclinations other than those necessary to manage a library effectively.

What, if any, is relevant non–public library experience?

Parker: I believe that non–public library experience in government and business, for example, is very relevant experience for library directors.

Raz: Academic library, state library, school library, cooperative or system library, and management experience in another field.

Skowronski: Comparable academic library experience in administration.

Zyskowski: I feel that any management or supervisory experience is relevant and should make a candidate more attractive. Also experience in technology would be especially relevant to a director's position.

Are there any degree expectations? Should they attend leadership institutes?

Parker: Advanced degree work at the master's level should be expected, but I think we will see library directors within the next five years without the MLS degrees, but with other relevant education.

Raz: MLS; public administration also helpful; evidence of *leadership* in the profession at state and national levels useful—not just participation.

Skowronski: Minimum degree required is an MLIS; an advanced degree is a plus.

Zyskowski: Certainly the person moving into a directorship will be required to have a degree from an accredited library school. A master's degree in business administration (MBA) or master's degree in public administration (MPA) would also not hurt. I do not, however, feel that participation in leadership institutes is important or relevant.

Is the Delphi list of desirable attributes comprehensive/complete?

Parker: I think the list reflects the librarian's penchant for lists and is way too long. Many of the attributes could be collapsed. For example: "able to work effectively with a variety of people from many constituencies" could replace all of the questions regarding ability to work effectively with friends, staff, boards, etc.

Raz: I do like these lists. I would add: "able to handle multiple tasks and projects," "able to work with a diverse staff and public," and "delegates authority and responsibility," which is a critical skill for a good director. Delegating authority means handing off to others and holding them responsible for getting the job done.

Skowronski: No—add risk taking.

Zyskowski: I would add a few comments to the Delphi list. Under personal attributes I feel that it is very important for a person aspiring to a directorship to have ambition. Another way to state this is that the person strives to be "the best" possible and is driven by the desire for achievement. In general I thought that the list was not consistent. That is to say it listed some traits or abilities that are very broad and conceptual in nature. It also, however, listed specific skills. I am not certain that the list was as effective as it could be in that sense. For example, one category is "able to work effectively with the staff." This is a very broad category encompassing a whole host of skills. I think you need to decide whether you want to list broad categories or whether you want to list specific skills that should be under those broad categories. You have listed "has good team building skills." It seems to me that this should be a subset of "able to work effectively with staff." So I tend to find the list somewhat inconsistent in theme. Also some of the items under managerial attributes seem so trivial as to be too unimportant to list. For example, "has a good sense of when to pitch in" or "has good time management skills."

Which attributes are most important? (Please limit these to a few from each category or about fifteen total.)

Parker:
- Able to work well with others (all listed);
- Able to communicate effectively (all listed);
- Advocate for the library;
- Able to be an innovative leader;
- Has integrity;
- Able to motivate/inspire;
- Financial literacy;
- Law and public policy issues relevant to public libraries; and
- Demographic and economic changes in the local, state, and regional communities.

Raz:
Managerial attributes

- Able to develop long-range plans in collaboration with library's community ("Creating a vision and a long-range plan *really works*. It is essential in guiding the board and staff and in communicating with the public.");
- Able to work effectively with staff;
- Able to work effectively with library boards;

- Has progressive administrative/managerial/supervisory experience; and
- Able to work effectively with state and local public officials.

Personal attributes

- Has a vision of the vital role that the library plays in the community;
- Able to demonstrate innovative leadership;
- Able to motivate staff;
- Is comfortable with diverse populations;
- Demonstrates excellent interpersonal/people skills; and
- Demonstrates effective oral and written communication skills.

Areas of knowledge

- Long-term planning;
- Budgeting and financial planning;
- Trends and innovations in libraries;
- Law and public policy issues relevant to public libraries; and
- Functions of library boards.

Skowronski:
Managerial attributes

- Ability to work with boards;
- Ability to work effectively with community/civic organizations; and
- Good team-building skills.

Personal attributes

- Integrity;
- Vision;
- Comfort; and
- Diversity.

Areas of knowledge

- Trends and innovations; and
- Long-term planning.

Zyskowski:
- Able to work effectively with library boards;
- Able to work effectively with staff;

- Able to articulate/communicate the vital role of the library to the community;
- Able to work effectively with state and local public officials;
- Able to integrate technology into the library;
- Has a vision of the role that the library plays in the community;
- Exhibits a strong commitment to public services;
- Trends and innovations in libraries;
- Current library practices;
- Budgeting and financial planning;
- Business administration; and
- Emerging technological trends.

Do you want to add/delete anything from the list?

Parker:
(She has already indicated where she would collapse portions of the list.)
Add:

- Being aware of customer service trends and innovations in the wider marketplace with possible application in public libraries. For example, supermarkets, airlines, and web-based retailers.
- Identify and recruit talent into strategic positions.
- Have serious sense of curiosity.

Raz:
Add:

- Ability to recognize talented staff and get them involved and excited; and
- Ability to create the "major vision" and keep focusing on it.

Zyskowski: My goal would not be necessarily to add or delete things other than the comments mentioned above. Rather it would be more effective groupings. The list seems haphazard and just thrown together. There should be broad categories with subsets under those broad categories to make the list more meaningful to deal with. [See chapter 6 where the authors attempt to do just that.]

Do you expect any changes in the necessary knowledge and skills for the future?

Parker: I hope so! I hope that the public library continues to be at the forefront of local, state, and federal economic and policy issues and that we maintain, gain, or recover our place as respected and trusted community resources. Directors need to be flexible and learn to keep their options open.

Raz: In the past ten years issues such as Internet pornography, filtering, major library construction projects, USF (Universal Services Fund), and technology issues have been very challenging. But regardless of what the future holds, the same basic skills for managers will continue to apply. The director does not need technology skills, just as she never needed cataloging skills. But hiring the right staff for the job that needs doing is the important skill for the director. Get good people and give them room to bloom and the organization will grow and grow. It is not just the director, but the talents of the staff that truly make the organization move ahead.

Skowronski: More reliance on ability to work with, recruit, and develop a diverse staff to work with a diverse customer base.

Zyskowski: I would expect a basic knowledge of how to manage organizations will always be a responsibility of the library director. In the future I would see an increased knowledge of technology being important for a library director. Although there will be staff to deal with these issues, the library director will have to make decisions based on a relatively high degree of knowledge.

What is your perception of the existing pool of candidates for directorships? Do they tend to have the desirable traits?

Parker: I have never hired a director, but I have worked for several. I find those with the broadest view possible of what the public library stands for to be the most effective leaders.

Raz: We need more specific training in management and leadership skills. We must encourage more women to pursue directorships. Directors need to mentor obviously talented individuals.

Zyskowski: In this area, and in the organizations I am familiar with, it is difficult to see these traits exhibited on the part of deputy directors. That is simply because I do not have that much contact with them. I am personally aware of a few deputies who possess many of these traits, but in their current capacities they would not be called upon to exercise or develop other traits.

Do boards of trustees have the same or different expectations for the successful candidate?

Parker: I truly believe that boards will hire directors for the present time and will not be looking to make a hire that will reach fifteen to twenty years into the future. Different experiences and skills are needed at different times and boards are bringing business expectations to the director's role. I do not think boards of the future will hesitate to hire a director, as needed, for the long-term good of the library community.

Raz: Boards should pay more attention to experience, track record, knowledge, and in-depth reference checking (a visit to last place of employment) and less attention to personality, charisma, and weight of one interview.

Zyskowski: I tend to think the question of boards of trustees varies from organization to organization. What they are looking for is often amazingly divergent and incredibly unsophisticated. Frequently decisions are based on issues related to personality rather than abilities.

In your opinion, why would someone want to become the director of a large or medium-sized public library?

Parker: I can only answer for myself. I have a personal debt to libraries and library staff for my development as a young person. Public library service is a great challenge and responsibility and should be taken very seriously.

Raz: It is a *great* job, full of headaches, busy as hell, always changing, with lots of surprises. It is dealing with staff members who have a rainbow of personalities, board members who can be challenging and difficult, politicians who do not have a clue, and usually a public that expects million-dollar service for a pittance of tax support. So, why wouldn't anyone want to jump right in? But if you want variety every day and can stick to a vision and long-range plan, want a job that is always changing, almost always exciting, and most days you cannot wait to get to work, well . . . this is it!

Skowronski: Myriad opportunities, salary, budgets sufficient to work with.

Zyskowski: I think the main motivation to wish to become a director of a large or medium-sized public library should have to do with the desire to accomplish something positive. Of course there are always ego matters as well as financial issues. However I would wish to find a director who really had a desire to accomplish something in his or her library.

Any other comments?

Parker: While I am a traditionalist in that my professional education is that of a librarian, my state and national associations offer me very little in the way of developing skills that I need every day to manage and lead effectively in a fast-paced, political environment. Library directors of the future will be looking outside the profession for models of success.

CONCLUSION

The participants in the Delphi study eventually generated a list of sixty-four items in three categories: managerial attributes, personal attributes, and areas of knowledge. The top-ranked managerial attributes tend to emphasize the director's ability to work with other groups and individuals (library boards, library staff, community and governmental agencies, friends' groups, and public officials). So not surprisingly, communication skills are deemed important. Integrity tops the list of personal attributes, but vision and communication skills also get high marks. A theme for the areas of knowledge is not apparent. Highly rated attributes include knowledge of trends and innovations, current library practices, long-term planning, financial management, and intellectual freedom.

Four representative directors of large and medium-sized public libraries provided written reactions to the final list of attributes. Their comments indicated a general satisfaction with the list, but they did emphasize five qualities more than did the participants in the Delphi study. Those five attributes were (1) director's ability to work effectively with a diverse staff; (2) director's ability to work effectively with a diverse public; (3) the importance of the director's being an innovative leader; (4) the need for strong communication skills; and (5) the need for the director to have a vision for the library.

Ellen Altman, past editor of *Public Libraries* and an educator, also provided a reaction to the final list of attributes. She expressed surprise over two attributes not included in the list—fundraising from the private sector/grantsmanship and cooperative work with the state library and other libraries in the area. Interestingly, grant writing and fundraising were in the initial list of attributes, but participants in the first round of the Delphi study recommended deleting them. Altman recommended adding: communicating the library's role to government; dealing with complaints and criticisms; creating visibility in the community; and being comfortable with diverse personalities, unhappy patrons, etc.

One of the items that made Corbus's list of key attributes is "good judgment."[3] That quality is not explicit in the final list generated by this study, but it may be at least partially covered by such attributes as "ability to engage in effective problem solving" and "has a good sense of when to pitch in."

At least two caveats, one of which is mentioned elsewhere in this book, are also in order. One is that directors' attributes may well vary in their relative importance from community to community and from library to library. The authors believe that the final list does represent a strong consensus, and many of the attributes are generic enough to apply to many situations; but certain attributes, especially the more specific ones, will be more important in some settings than in others. As Altman pointed out, a number of attributes begin with the words "is willing," but, unfortunately, one may be willing but not effective. With that in mind, chapter 7 addresses the issues of self-assessment of leadership qualities and the means for strengthening them.

> The many issues that face public libraries at present and in future require effective leadership in terms of developing and promoting vision,...[identifying] priorities, handling competitors, and providing information services needed by a changing, diverse, and increasingly technological savvy user population.[4]

NOTES

1. Reed Osborne, "Evaluation of Leadership in Ontario Public Libraries," *Canadian Journal of Information and Library Science* 21 (September–December 1996): 21.
2. Laurence Corbus, "Key Attributes for Library Administration," *Public Libraries* 37, no. 6 (November–December 1998): 355–56.
3. Ibid.
4. Mark D. Winston and Teresa Y. Neely, "Leadership Development and Public Libraries," *Public Library Quarterly* 19 (2001): 15–16.

6

ANALYSIS AND COMPARISON OF QUALITIES

[G]reat leaders[.] As you read…[those] words…, what came to mind?[1]

This chapter takes the qualities listed in Tables 3.1, 4.1, and 5.1 (covering directors of academic libraries that belong to the Association of Research Libraries, other academic libraries, and public libraries), and it offers comparisons along with a consolidation and regrouping of the three sets of qualities. The purpose of the regroupings in this chapter is to identify patterns and to make the lists more useful to the readers of this book. The chapter also sets up chapter 8, which discusses how the various qualities are best acquired.

ARL DIRECTORS

As explained in chapter 3, one of the ARL directors interviewed suggested that the qualities identified in Table 3.1 should be regrouped into four categories: (1) external/policy/ citizen of the university/campus; (2) resource development; (3) library culture; and (4) strategic direction. Library culture exists internally (the operation of the library), whereas the first and fourth categories have external dimensions and implications. Resource development might best be considered within the context of the other categories; these categories, most likely, shape the library's response to (and proactive efforts to manage and acquire) resources. Of course, resource development also has implications for the other areas as the library plots its strategic directions within the university or local government.

Figure 6.1, which assigns the qualities to the four categories, indicates that, although the qualities tend to coalesce in the first and third categories, the fourth category is well represented. Even though resource development

Figure 6.1
Qualities Grouped by Topical Areas (ARL Libraries)

Qualities	External/Policy/ Citizen of University/Campus	Resource Development	Library Culture	Strategic Direction
Is committed to service			X	X
Is results oriented		X	X	X
Communicates effectively with staff			X	
Delegates authority			X	
Facilitates a productive work environment			X	
Is willing to make tough decisions			X	
Promotes professional growth in staff			X	
Manages fiscal resources/budgets			X	
Engages in fundraising and donor relations		X		
Nurtures the development of new programs and services/refines existing ones as needed			X	X
Develops various sources of funding		X		
Is committed to staff diversity (and is culturally sensitive)			X	
Ensures that planned action is implemented and evaluated			X	
Facilitates the group process			X	
Resolves conflicts			X	
Builds a shared vision for the library	X			
Manages/shapes change			X	
Is able to function in a political environment	X			
Develops a campus visibility for the library	X			
Is an advocate for librarians' role in higher education	X			
Thinks "outside the box" (in new and creative ways applicable to the problem)			X	
Builds consensus in carrying out strategic directions			X	X
Leads and participates in consortia and cooperative endeavors				X
Is collaborative	X		X	
Is entrepreneurial		X		
Brings issues of broad importance to the university community, fostering wide discussion and action, when appropriate	X			
Demonstrates effective networking skills				X
Keeps the library focused on its mission			X	
Changes/shapes the library's culture			X	
Develops and fosters partnerships with groups and organizations on/off campus	X			
Leads in a shared decision-making environment	X			
Sets priorities			X	
Plans for life cycles of information technologies and services			X	
Responds to needs of various constituencies				X
Creates and implements systems that assess the library's value to its users				X

Figure 6.1
Qualities Grouped by Topical Areas (ARL Libraries) (continued)

Creates an environment that fosters accountability			X	
Has credibility			X	
Is evenhanded			X	
Is self-confident			X	
Is accessible			X	
Treats people with dignity/respect			X	
Is able to work effectively in groups			X	
Is articulate	X		X	X
Has a sense of perspective			X	
Is diplomatic			X	
Is open-minded			X	
Is a good listener			X	
Is able to compromise			X	X
Has a sense of humor	X		X	
Has good interpersonal/people skills	X		X	
Is committed to a set of values (integrity)			X	
Is able to handle stress	X		X	
Works on multiple tasks simultaneously			X	
Is comfortable with ambiguity			X	
Is committed to job and profession	X		X	
Has self-awareness of strengths and weaknesses			X	
Is honest			X	
Is energetic	X		X	
Is resilient	X		X	
Analyzes and solves problems			X	
Has a variety of work experiences			X	
Is able "to think on one's feet"—"wing it"			X	
Is intuitive			X	
Has a broad knowledge of issues	X		X	
Is able to ask the right questions			X	
Manages time effectively			X	
Exercises good judgment	X		X	
Articulates direction for the library			X	X
Inspires trust	X		X	
Is innovative			X	
Has organizational agility			X	
Is persuasive			X	
Has reasonable risk-taking skills		X	X	
Is optimistic	X		X	
Understands that one does not have all the answers			X	
Is enthusiastic	X		X	
Is an enabler and facilitator			X	
Is committed to learning from mistakes		X	X	
Takes initiative	X		X	
Has team-building skills			X	
Is committed to explaining decisions			X	
Scholarly communication	X	X	X	X
Understands the complex environment in which the library functions			X	
Knowledge of financial management			X	
Facilities planning (including remote storage and multi-use buildings)			X	

Figure 6.1
Qualities Grouped by Topical Areas (ARL Libraries) (continued)

Digital libraries		X	X	
Planning (strategic, longterm)				X
Trends in higher education	X			
Information technology	X	X	X	X
Management issues			X	
Outcomes (and accreditation) assessment	X		X	X
User expectations/information needs	X		X	X
Intellectual property rights	X		X	X
Fundraising		X		
Community's view of the library	X			X
Public relations	X			X
Service quality measurement			X	X
Goals (educational, research, and service) of the parent institution	X			
Information delivery systems			X	
Publishing industry		X	X	
Resource sharing				X
Information literacy			X	X
Teaching and learning theory			X	

produced the fewest number of qualities, this category remains vital to the performance of many library directors, given the particular qualities that belong here.

The Center for Creative Leadership (see chapter 7) offers a number of leadership assessment tools, some of which group qualities into ten thematic areas and subareas. To gain another perspective on the qualities discovered in the research, we grouped them into similar thematic areas and the appropriate subareas (conceivably, a quality might appear in more than one grouping):

1. Organizational/Institutional Leadership
   Mission/Vision
      Builds a shared vision for the library
      Develops a campus visibility for the library
      Is an advocate for librarian's role in higher education
      Keeps the library focused on its mission
      Leads in a shared decision-making environment
      Understands the complex environment in which the library functions
      Is able to function in a political environment
      Articulates direction for the library
   Planning and Goal Setting
      Builds consensus in carrying out strategic directions
      Changes/shapes the library's culture

    Planning (strategic, long-term)

    Plans for life cycles of information technologies and services

  Issue Awareness

    Brings issues of broad importance to the university community, fostering wide discussion and action, when appropriate

  Change Management

    Manages/shapes change

2. Problem Solving and Decision Making

  Problem Solving

    Analyzes and solves problems

  Taking Action and Following through

    Is results oriented

    Is willing to make tough decisions

    Ensures that planned action is implemented and evaluated

3. Risk, Innovation, and Adaptability

  Risk taking

    Has reasonable risk-taking skills

  Innovation

    Thinks "outside the box" (in new and creative ways applicable to the problem)

    Is entrepreneurial

    Is innovative

    Exercises good judgment

  Flexibility

    Has organizational agility

4. Business Knowledge and Skills

  Knowledge Areas

    Has a broad knowledge of issues (the general knowledge areas in Table 3.1)

  Customer Relations

    Is committed to service

    Responds to needs of various constituencies

    Creates and implements systems that assess the library's value to its users

  Financial Management

    Manages fiscal resources/budgets

Program Development

    Nurtures the development of new programs and services/refines existing ones as needed

Resource Development

    Develops various sources of funding

    Engages in fundraising and donor relations

5. Communication

    Communicates effectively with staff

    Is articulate

    Has good interpersonal/people skills

    Is able to "think on one's feet"—"wing it"

    Is persuasive

Listening

    Is a good listener

6. Developing People and Managing the Work of Others

Leading Employees

    Facilitates a productive work environment

    Is collaborative

    Sets priorities

    Creates an environment that fosters accountability

    Is accessible

    Is committed to explaining decisions

    Is able to work effectively in groups

    Has team-building skills

Motivating Others

    Promotes professional growth in staff

Organizing

    Facilitates the group process

Delegating

    Delegates authority

Diversity

    Is committed to staff diversity (and is culturally sensitive)

7. Building and Maintaining Relations

Relationships

    Leads and participates in consortia and cooperative endeavors

Develops and fosters partnerships with groups and organizations on/off campus

Managing Conflict

Resolves conflicts

8. Integrity/Values/Drive/Personal Conduct

Ethics/Culture/Integrity

Has credibility

Is committed to a set of values (integrity)

Is honest

Inspires trust

Drive and Purpose

Is an enabler and facilitator

Takes initiative

Personal Conduct

Is evenhanded

Is self-confident

Treats people with dignity/respect

Has a sense of perspective

Is diplomatic

Is open-minded

Is able to compromise

Has a sense of humor

Is committed to job and profession

Is energetic

Is resilient

Is intuitive

Is enthusiastic

Is optimistic

9. Management of One's Self

Coping with Pressure

Is able to handle stress

Time Management

Works on multiple tasks simultaneously

Manages time effectively

10. Self-Awareness, Development, and Learning

   Self-Awareness

      Has self-awareness of strengths and weaknesses

      Understands that one does not have all the answers

      Is comfortable with ambiguity

   Self-Management (including Opportunities to Learn)

      Has a variety of work experiences

   Learns from Mistakes

      Is committed to learning from mistakes

ACRL LIBRARY DIRECTORS

Figure 6.2 groups the qualities for other academic library directors into the same broad categories as depicted in Figure 6.1, and once again the first and third categories are the most heavily populated. The following grouping offers a characterization of the list relying on the thematic areas and subareas developed by the Center for Creative Leadership. The grouping in this section, however, results in the creation of two new thematic areas: work experience and degrees held.

1. Leadership (at the Organizational/Institutional Level)

   Mission/Vision

      Understands and is committed to institutional mission

      Has vision in formulating programs and implementing strategies to integrate print and electronic resources

      Is able to serve as an advocate for the library

      Is able to articulate vision for library within the institution

      Has experience with public relations

      Has proven ability to foster community building

   Planning and Goal Setting

      Is able to plan, implement, and assess strategic goals

      Has experience with long-range planning

      Has experience with collaborative arrangements between/among multicampus and statewide settings and other institutions

      Has experience with facilities planning

      Has experience managing or planning digital libraries

      Has experience in planning or coordinating new library building projects

Figure 6.2
Qualities Grouped by Topical Areas (ACRL Libraries)

Qualities	External/Policy/ Citizen of University/Campus	Resource Development	Library Culture	Strategic Direction
Has supervisory experience			X	
Has proven managerial ability in personnel, fiscal, budgetary, and program assessment matters		X	X	
Is able to plan, implement, and evaluate strategic goals				X
Is able to work in collegial, networked environment			X	
Understands and is committed to institutional mission				X
Has proven facilitative leadership skills	X		X	
Has proven ability to foster team building and participatory management			X	
Has a record of innovative and effective leadership	X		X	
Has firm commitment to quality	X		X	
Has a vision in formulating programs and implementing strategies to integrate print and electronic resources				X
Has experience in positions of increasing responsibility			X	
Is committed to diversity			X	
Has demonstrated ability to identify trends				X
Has experience in developing digital libraries			X	X
Has integrity			X	
Strong interpersonal skills	X		X	
Is able to serve as an advocate for library (develops, articulates, and communicates a rationale for the library)	X			
Has excellent oral and written communication skills	X		X	
Is able to work collaboratively with campus colleagues	X			
Is able to articulate vision for library within the institution				X
Has demonstrated ability to exercise mature judgment			X	
Has MLS			X	
Is flexible			X	
Has good listening skills	X		X	
Is committed to professional development of library personnel			X	
Respects scholarship, learning, and teaching	X		X	X
Has strong service orientation			X	X

Note: This figure includes changes in the wording of items, as well as adds some new items, resulting from the research reported in chapter 8.

Figure 6.2
Qualities Grouped by Topical Areas (ACRL Libraries) (continued)

Shows enthusiasm for work in an educational environment	X		X	
Has a sense of humor	X		X	
Has a documented record of problem solving			X	
Is creative			X	
Has a high energy level	X		X	
Is dynamic	X		X	
Has an advanced degree (other than MLS)			X	
Has knowledge of library operations			X	
Has experience with change management			X	
Has experience with current technology and information systems as they apply to libraries	X	X	X	X
Has experience with program assessment and evaluation	X		X	
Has experience with information technology	X	X	X	X
Has experience with planning: strategic, technology, collection development, marketing, facilities, security, personnel development, and fundraising			X	X
Has experience with collaborative arrangements between/among multicampus and statewide settings and other institutions	X		X	X
Has experience with scholarly communication	X	X	X	X
Has experience with public relations	X			X
Has knowledge of collection development			X	
Has experience with marketing of services and resources	X		X	X
Has record of scholarly achievement	X		X	
Has proven ability to foster community building	X		X	X
Has proven fundraising capabilities and success in securing funding support		X		
Has experience with information literacy	X		X	X
Has knowledge of bibliographic control			X	
Has experience in managing or planning digital libraries	X	X	X	X
Has experience with grant writing		X		X
Has experience in planning or coordinating new library building projects			X	X
Has expertise with distance education	X	X	X	X
Is committed to the principles of resource sharing among all types of libraries			X	X

Issue and Trend Awareness

    Has demonstrated ability to identify trends

Change Management

    Has experience with change management

2. Problem Solving and Decision Making

  Problem Solving

    Has demonstrated ability to exercise mature judgment

    Has a documented record of problem solving

3. Risk, Innovation, and Adaptability

  Flexibility

    Is flexible

4. Business Knowledge and Skills

  Knowledge Areas

    Has respect for scholarship and learning

    Has knowledge of

      library operations

      bibliographic control (see also no. 11, Experience [Work and Scholarship])

  Customer Relations

    Has firm commitment to quality

    Has strong service orientation

  Financial Management

    Has proven managerial ability in personnel, fiscal, budgetary, and program matters

  Program Development

    Has proven managerial ability in personnel, fiscal, budgetary, and program matters

    Has experience with scholarly communication

    Has experience with marketing of services and resources

    Has expertise with distance education

  Resource Development

    Has experience with marketing of services and resources

    Has proven fundraising capabilities and success in securing funding support

    Has experience with grant writing

5. Communication

> Has strong interpersonal skills
>
> Has excellent oral and written communication skills

Listening

> Has good listening skills

6. Developing People and Managing the Work of Others

> Is committed to professional development of library personnel

Leading Employees

> Has supervisory experience
>
> Has proven facilitative leadership skills
>
> Has a record of innovative and effective leadership

Organizing

> Has proven managerial ability in personnel, fiscal, budgetary, and program matters
>
> Has proven ability to foster team building and participatory management

Diversity

> Is committed to diversity

Collaboration

> Is able to work collaboratively with campus colleagues
>
> Has experience with collaborative arrangements between/among multicampus and statewide settings and other institutions

7. Building and Maintaining Relations

> Is able to work in collegial, networked environment
>
> Has experience with collaborative arrangements between/among multicampus and statewide settings and other institutions

8. Integrity/Values/Drive/Personal Conduct

Ethics/Culture/Integrity

> Has integrity

Personal Conduct

> Has a sense of humor
>
> Is creative
>
> Has high energy level
>
> Is dynamic

9. Management of One's Self

> (none)

10. Self-Awareness, Development, and Learning

    Self-Management (including Opportunities to Learn)

    Is enthusiastic about working in an educational environment

11. Experience (Work and Scholarship)

    Has experience in positions of increasing responsibility

    Has experience with

    change management

    current technology and information systems as they apply to libraries

    program assessment and evaluation

    long-range planning

    collaborative arrangements between/among multicampus and state-wide settings and other institutions

    scholarly communication

    public relations

    collection development

    marketing of services and resources

    information literacy

    managing or planning digital libraries

    developing digital libraries

    Has record of scholarly achievement

12. Degrees

    Has MLS

    Has a second advanced degree

PUBLIC LIBRARY DIRECTORS

Figure 6.3, which is also similar to figures 6.1 and 6.2, shows that public library directors are less involved with resource development. However, it merits mention that, in the last couple of years, a number of job advertisements for public library directors call for competency in fundraising. It is also apparent that a number of qualities are similar (e.g., "is able to work effectively with library boards" and "functions of library boards," or is able to work effectively with stakeholders and constituency groups, be they library boards, community/civic and governmental agencies/organizations, friends' groups, unions, individual constituencies, or the general public).

A second perspective is gained from grouping the qualities into the thematic areas and the various subareas advanced by the Center for Creative Leadership:

Figure 6.3
Qualities Grouped by Topical Areas (Public Libraries)

Qualities	External/Policy/ Citizen of University/Campus	Resource Development	Library Culture	Strategic Direction
Is able to work effectively with library boards	X			
Is able to communicate effectively with staff			X	
Is able to work effectively with staff			X	
Is an advocate for the library with (1) community/civic and (2) government agencies/organizations	X			
Is able to articulate/communicate the vital role of the library to the community and to government	X			
Is able to engage in effective problem solving			X	
Is able to work effectively with community/civic organizations	X			
Is able to work effectively with friends' groups	X			
Is able to work effectively with state and local public officials	X			
Is willing to involve staff in planning and development of services			X	
Is able to develop long-range plans in collaboration with library's community	X			X
Has good team-building skills			X	
Is willing to further the professional development of staff			X	
Is willing to encourage board and other community members to be advocates	X			
Is able to work effectively with a union	X		X	X
Advocates for the library with individual constituents	X			
Is able to work effectively with the general public	X			
Has good time-management skills			X	
Has good understanding of job assignments and workflow			X	
Appreciates importance of marketing/public relations	X			X
Is able to manage all facets of library operations			X	
Has progressive administrative/managerial/supervisory experience			X	
Is able to integrate technology into the library			X	
Has a good sense of when to pitch in			X	
Has an appropriate number of years of professional experience (reflecting progressive managerial responsibilities)			X	
Is able to design outreach services			X	X
Has integrity			X	

Note: This figure includes changes in the wording of items, as well as adds some new items, resulting from the research reported in chapter 8.

Figure 6.3
Qualities Grouped by Topical Areas (Public Libraries) (continued)

Has a vision of the vital role that the library plays in the community	X			
Demonstrates effective oral and written communication skills	X		X	
Demonstrates excellent interpersonal/people skills	X		X	
Exhibits a strong commitment to public service			X	X
Is comfortable with diverse populations	X		X	
Has good collaborative skills	X		X	
Is able to motivate/inspire staff			X	
Has good organizational skills			X	
Projects a professional manner	X		X	
Is able to demonstrate innovative leadership	X		X	
Furthers own professional development			X	
Is active professionally			X	
Engages in community service	X			
Trends and innovations in libraries			X	
Current library practices			X	
Long-term planning			X	
Budgeting and financial planning		X	X	
Intellectual freedom	X		X	X
Law and public policy issues relevant to public libraries	X			X
Demographic changes in the community				X
Economic changes in the community				X
Functions of library boards	X			
Roles of state/local public officials	X			
Business administration			X	
Functions of friends' groups	X			
Knowledge of the general public	X			
Community analysis				X
Emerging technological trends				X
Building and remodeling			X	
Concepts of collection development			X	
Project management			X	
Current human resources administration/personnel administration			X	
Measurement and evaluation methods			X	
Library public services			X	
Library technical services			X	
Trends and innovations in education				X
Major foreign language(s) of community	X			X
Fundraising		X		
Has experience with grant writing		X		
Works well with state library and other libraries in the area on cooperative projects to improve service			X	
Is committed to the principles of resource sharing among all types of libraries			X	X

1. Leadership (at the Organizational/Institutional Level)
    Mission/Vision
        Advocates for the library with community/civic and governmental agencies/organizations
        Is able to articulate/communicate the vital role of the library to the community
        Is able to work effectively with community/civic organizations
        Is able to work effectively with friends' groups
        Is able to work effectively with state and local public officials
        Is able to work effectively with a union
        Advocates for the library with individual constituents
        Has a vision of the vital role that the library plays in the community
    Planning and Goal Setting
        Is willing to involve staff in planning and development of services
        Is able to develop long-range plans in collaboration with library's community
        Is able to integrate technology into the library
        Has a strong commitment to public services
    Dealing with Others
        Is able to work effectively with library boards
        Is able to work effectively with the general public
        Is comfortable with diverse populations
2. Problem Solving and Decision Making
    Problem Solving
        Is able to engage in effective problem solving
3. Innovation
        Is able to demonstrate innovative leadership
4. Business Knowledge and Skills
    Knowledge Areas
        Appreciates importance of marketing/public relations (the general areas of knowledge specified in Figure 6.3)
5. Communication
        Demonstrates effective oral and written communication skills
        Demonstrates excellent interpersonal/people skills
6. Developing People and Managing the Work of Others
    Leading Employees

Is able to communicate effectively with staff

Is able to work effectively with staff

Has good team-building skills

Motivating Others

Is willing to further the professional development of staff

Is able to motivate/inspire staff

Organizing

Has a good sense of when to pitch in

Is able to design outreach services

Has good organization skills

7. Integrity/Values/Drive/Personal Conduct

Ethics/Culture/Integrity

Has integrity

Personal Conduct

Has good collaborative skills

Projects a professional manner

Is active professionally

Has a willingness to engage in community service

8. Management of One's Self

Time Management

Has good time-management skills

9. Self-Awareness, Development, and Learning

Self-Awareness

Has good understanding of job assignments and workflow

Is able to manage all facets of library operations

Has progressive administrative/managerial/supervisory experience

Has an appropriate number of years of professional experience

Self-Management (including Opportunities to Learn)

Is willing to further own professional development

COMBINED LIST

This section offers some general observations about the lists of qualities for ARL, other academic library, and public library directors already reported in this chapter. It also combines the three lists into one list and regroups the assorted items into related categories. The purpose of the combined list—and its characterization—is to offer yet another view of how the qualities might be displayed. As a result, readers have another choice for making sense—or practical use—of the qualities identified in this and preceding chapters.

Comparison

From an examination of the lists generated using the scheme developed by the Center for Creative Leadership, it is evident that the qualities for academic library directors correspond well to ten thematic areas. However, for non–ARL library directors, two additional areas appear, "Experience (Work and Scholarship)" and "Degrees." The list for public library directors parallels nine of the ten thematic areas; "Building and Maintaining Relations" was absent. Theme three, which focused exclusively on "innovation" and "risk and adaptability," was only minimally represented.

Finally, the list of qualities for ARL directors was the longest, followed by the list for public library directors and then for non–ARL academic library directors. Naturally, there are variations among subareas reported for the three lists; however, the analysis presented in this section does not identify differences among the subareas. Such detail is not necessary as the purpose is to make the lists more practical—to enable readers to identify the subset on which they want to focus their attention or that of others.

Combined List

Table 6.1 presents the items listed in the previous three figures in this chapter as a consolidated list. Even though the exact wording of a quality might be specific to a type of library, it was easy to find some commonality among the lists. A good example relates to the director as an advocate for the library and as someone who interacts well with different constituencies and other groups (be they, for instance, library boards or the upper administration of a college or university). By using a qualitative data analysis product, *The Ethnograph v5.0*™ (Sage Publications Software: Scolari),[2] that list was further refined (see Figure 6.4). For each of the categories identified in the figure, Table 6.2 lists those categories and the individual qualities that correspond to each category. As a result, readers can see where each individual item falls within the combined list.[3]

An examination of Table 6.2 indicates that

- The largest category (i.e., the one with the most qualities) is, by far, "Knowledge Areas (Professional Issues)";
- The largest subcategory is "Management" under "Knowledge Areas—Professional Issues)";
- The five largest categories are, from highest to lowest, "Knowledge Areas (Professional Issues)", "Professional Presence," "Productive Work Environment,"

Table 6.1
Combined List of Qualities

Management

Ability to foster team building and participatory management
Ability in personnel, fiscal, budgetary, and program matters
Appropriate number of years of professional experience
Communicates effectively with staff
Creates and implements systems that assess the library's value to its users
Delegates authority
Designs outreach services
Develops digital libraries
Engages in effective problem solving
Ensures that planned action is implemented and evaluated
Experience in positions of increasing responsibility
Facilitates a productive work environment (including teamwork and the group
  process)
Good team-building skills
Involves staff in planning and development of services
Integrates technology into the library (plans for life cycles of information
  technologies and services)
Is committed to the principles of resource sharing among all types of libraries
Makes tough decisions
Manages all facets of library operations (including fiscal resources/budgets)
Manages/shapes change
Nurtures the development of new programs and services/refines existing ones as
  needed
Resolves conflicts
Understands job assignments and workflow
Works effectively with staff, constituency groups, and union

Leadership

Ability to identify trends
Ability to plan, implement, and assess strategic goals
Ability to work in collegial, networked environment
Advocate for library
Appreciates importance of marketing/public relations
Articulates/communicates the vital role of the library to the community
Articulates direction for the library
Brings issues of broad importance to the university community, fostering wide
  discussion and action, when appropriate
Builds a shared vision for the library
Builds consensus in carrying out strategic directions
Changes/shapes the library's culture
Collaborative skills (works collaboratively with campus colleagues)
Commitment to (and record on) staff diversity (as well as comfortable with diverse
  populations and is culturally sensitive)
Commitment to professional development of library personnel
Creates an environment that fosters accountability

Table 6.1
Combined List of Qualities (continued)

Leadership (continued)

Demonstrates innovative leadership
Develops a campus visibility for the library
Develops long-range plans in collaboration with library's community
Develops various sources of funding
Develops and fosters partnerships with groups and organizations on/off campus
Encourages others (board and other community members) to be advocates for the
 library
Engages in fundraising and donor relations
Exercise mature judgment
Facilitative leadership skills
Functions in a political environment
Keeps the library focused on its mission
Leads in a shared decision-making environment
Leads and participates in consortia and cooperative endeavors
Motivates/inspires staff
Problem solver
Record of innovative and effective leadership
Responds to needs of various constituencies
Thinks "outside the box" (in new and creative ways applicable to the problem)
Understanding and commitment to institutional mission
Vision of the vital role that the library plays in the community
Work effectively with groups (e.g., library boards, friends' groups, community/civic
 organizations, and state and local public officials)
Vision in formulating programs and implementing strategies to integrate print and
 electronic resources

Personal Traits

Able to ask the right questions
Able to compromise
Able to handle stress
Able to "to think on one's feet"—"wing it"
Accessible
Active professionally
Analyzes and solves problems
Articulate
Comfortable with ambiguity
Commitment to quality
Committed to job and profession
Committed to a set of values (integrity)
Creative
Credibility
Diplomatic
Dynamic
Enabler and facilitator
Energetic

Table 6.1
Combined List of Qualities (continued)

Personal Traits (continued)

Engages in community service
Enthusiasm for work in an educational environment
Entrepreneurial
Evenhanded
Exercises good judgment
Explains decisions
Flexibility
High energy level
Honest
Innovative
Inspires trust
Integrity
Interpersonal and people skills
Intuitive
Learns from mistakes
Listening skills
Manages time effectively
Networking skills
Open-minded
Optimistic
Oral and written communication skills
Organizational agility
Organizational skills
Persuasive
Projects a professional manner
Reasonable risk-taking skills
Resilient
Respect for scholarship and learning
Results oriented
Self-awareness of strengths and weaknesses
Self-confident
Sense of humor
Sense of perspective
Sense of when to pitch in
Service orientation (commitment to public service)
Sets priorities
Takes initiative
Team-building skills
Treats people with dignity/respect
Understands that he/she does not have all the answers
Willing to further own professional development
Works on multiple tasks simultaneously

Table 6.1
Combined List of Qualities (continued)

Knowledge Areas

Bibliographic control
Budgeting and financial planning (fiscal management)
Change management
Collaborative arrangements between/among multicampus and statewide settings
    and other institutions
Collection development
Community analysis (including user expectations/information needs)
Community's view of the library
Coordinating new library building projects
Current human resources administration/personnel administration
Current library practices
Current technology and information systems as they apply to libraries
Demographic changes in the community
Designing library buildings and remodeling
Digital libraries, their management or planning
Distance education
Economic changes in the community
Emerging technological trends
Functions of library boards and friends' groups
Fundraising (successful)
Goals (educational, research, and service) of the parent institution
Good time-management skills
Grant writing
Information delivery systems
Information literacy
Information technology
Intellectual freedom
Intellectual property rights
Knowledge of the general public
Law and public policy issues relevant to public libraries
Library operations (including public and technical services)
Major foreign language(s) of community
Management issues
Marketing of services and resources
Measurement and evaluation methods (including service quality measurement and
    outcomes and accreditation assessment)
Planning, facilities (including remote storage and multi-use buildings), long-range,
    and strategic
Program assessment and evaluation
Project management
Public relations
Publishing industry
Resource sharing
Roles of state/local public officials

Table 6.1
Combined List of Qualities (continued)

<hr>

Knowledge Areas (continued)

Scholarly communication
Teaching and learning theory
Trends and innovations in education, higher and other
Trends and innovations in libraries
Understands the complex environment in which the library functions

Other

Broad knowledge of issues
Professional degree (MLS) and second advanced degree (ACRL)
Progressive administrative/managerial/supervisory experience (including variety of
    work experiences)
Record of scholarly achievement
Supervisory experience

<hr>

"Personal Characteristics (Internal Make-Up)," and a tie between "Leadership" and "Personal Characteristics (Dealing with Others)"; and

• The smallest categories were the four with only one quality each: "Staff growth," "Leadership (Donor Relations)," "Leadership (Image/Role Setting)," and "Educational Attainment."

It is difficult to identify any consistent themes in the figure broader than those represented by the listed categories; but it is interesting that being knowledgeable, a relatively traditional quality, was ranked so high and that technology received so little attention.

CONCLUSION

Acknowledging the criticism that the lists included in chapters 3 through 5 contained too many qualities and needed more effective regrouping, this chapter offers different groupings and conceptualizations of the lists of attributes. Figures 6.1 through 6.3 add important perspectives on the qualities identified through the use of the Delphi technique. Those lists reflect the director as an advocate for the library (dealing with constituent groups and other external forces) and as someone who shapes and manages the library's culture, sets the strategic direction of the library, and engages in resource development. As a generalization, it might be said that ARL library directors are the most likely to be involved in resource development and, in some instances, on a larger scale than their counterparts in other types of libraries. However, this is likely to change over time.

Undoubtedly, there are other ways to display the set of qualities generated by the research reported in previous chapters. Further research might com-

Figure 6.4
Conceptualization of the Thematic Areas Represented by the Qualities in Table 6.1

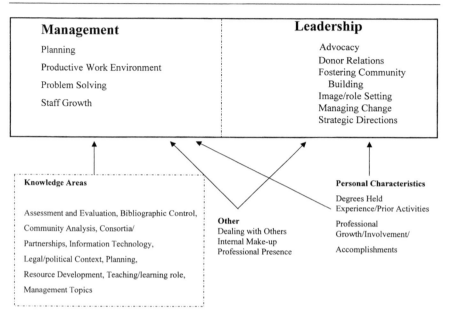

pare, more thoroughly, figures 6.1, 6.2, and 6.3, and quantify the results. For example, both ARL and other academic library directors mentioned their involvement in fundraising, whereas the subject only arose with public libraries during the final phase of the research—preparation of chapter 8, when additional leaders offered their perspective on the lists. How does fundraising differ, and how is it similar, across library types? It would also be interesting to gather feedback from college and university presidents, deans outside of librarianship, and library boards about the lists displayed in this chapter. Clearly, the qualities identified have a library focus, but can these other groups suggest additional qualities, and which ones do they consider most important (and in what circumstances)?

Finally, chapters 7 and 8 examine ways in which individuals can gain proficiency with a given set of qualities; chapter 8 reports perceptions of various leaders about which methods in general are best. Consequently, these chapters concentrate on the use of the tables reported in chapters 3 through 5, as well as the figures and tables in this chapter.

> The position of chief librarian may in fact be a very isolating one—never truly a peer or colleague of the librarians by virtue of the status of the position, nor one of the deans (who have their own cohort of other deans for support) and not one of the vice presidents or other executive administrators.[4]

No leader can *make* a team perform well. But all leaders can create conditions that increase the *likelihood* that it will.[5]

Table 6.2
Regrouping of the Qualities Displayed in Table 6.1

Planning (Establish/Follow Through)

Creates and implements systems that assess the library's value to its users

Designs outreach services

Develops digital libraries

Ensures that planned action is implemented and evaluated

Has experience with planning (strategic, technology [e.g., plans for life cycles of information technologies], collection development, marketing, facilities, security, personnel development, and fundraising)

Nurtures the development of new programs and services/refines existing ones as needed

Productive Work Environment

Ability in personnel, fiscal, budgetary, and program assessment matters

Ability to foster team building and participatory management

Applies, as appropriate, human resources policies from institution and government (local, county, state, and federal)

Comfortable with a wide range of user personalities (e.g., upset parents or irate faculty)

Commitment to (and record on) staff diversity (as well as is culturally sensitive)

Copes well with public's complaints and criticism of library collections/services

Creates an environment that fosters accountability

Delegates authority

Integrates technology effectively into the library

Involves staff in planning and development of services

Is committed to the principles of resource sharing among all types of libraries

Knowledgeable about all facets of library operations

Meets information needs of constituency groups

Motivates/inspires staff

Resolves conflicts

Understands job assignments and workflow

Works effectively with staff and union

Problem Solving

Able to ask the right questions

Engages in effective problem solving

Exercises mature, reasoned judgment

Thinks "outside the box" (in new and creative ways applicable to the problem)

Staff Growth

Commitment to professional development of library personnel

Leadership (Advocacy)

Develops, articulates, and communicates a rationale for library's role and services

Encourages others (board and other community members) to be advocates for the library

Inspires advocacy from nonadvocates

Table 6.2
Regrouping of the Qualities Displayed in Table 6.1 (continued)

Leadership (Donor Relations)
Engages in fundraising and donor relations

Leadership (Fostering Community Building)
Ability to work in collegial, networked environment

Brings issues of broad importance to the community, fostering wide discussion and
   action, when appropriate

Comfortable with diverse populations and is culturally sensitive

Communicates using multiplicity of formats

Functions in a political environment

Leads in a shared decision-making environment

Leads and participates in consortia and cooperative endeavors

Works collaboratively with community groups (e.g., faculty, library boards, friends'
   groups, community/civic organizations, and state and local public officials)

Works effectively with these groups

Leadership (Image/Role Setting)
Appreciates importance of marketing/public relations

Leadership (Direct Manage Change)
Changes/shapes the library's culture

Influences parent institution

Manages/shapes change

Leadership (Strategic Directions)
Ability to plan, implement, and evaluate strategic goals

Articulates/communicates the vital role of the library to the community

Articulates direction for the library

Builds a shared vision for the library

Builds consensus in carrying out strategic directions

Develops a campus visibility for the library

Develops and fosters partnerships with groups and organizations on/off campus

Develops various sources of funding

Has a vision for formulating programs and implementing strategies to integrate
   print and electronic resources

Involves library's community in planning (as needed)

Keeps the library focused on its mission

Understanding and commitment to institutional mission

Educational Attainment
Credentials: Professional degree (MLS) and second advanced degree (ACRL)

Experience/Prior Activities
Progressive administrative/managerial/supervisory experience (including variety of
   work experiences)

Record of innovative and effective leadership

Table 6.2
Regrouping of the Qualities Displayed in Table 6.1 (continued)

Professional Growth/Involvement/Accomplishment

Active professionally
Committed to job and profession
Furthers own professional development
Record of scholarly achievement

Professional Presence

Articulate
Available/accessible
Committed to a set of values (integrity)
Creative
Credibility
Diplomatic
Dynamic
Energetic
Engages in community service
Enthusiasm for work in an educational environment
Entrepreneurial
Honest
Innovative
Interpersonal and people skills
Listening skills
Oral and written communication skills
Organizational agility
Organizational skills
Optimistic
Persuasive
Projects a professional manner
Reasonable risk-taking skills
Resilient
Respect for scholarship, learning, and teaching
Results oriented
Sense of perspective

Personal Characteristics (Internal Make-Up)

Comfortable with ambiguity
Commitment to quality (collections/service)
Handles stress
Intuitive
Learns from mistakes
Makes tough decisions
Manages time effectively
Open-minded
Self-awareness of strengths and weaknesses
Self-confident
Sense of when to pitch in
Sets priorities

Table 6.2
Regrouping of the Qualities Displayed in Table 6.1 (continued)

Personal Characteristics (Internal Make-Up) (continued)

Takes initiative
Understands that he/she does not have all the answers
Works on multiple tasks simultaneously

Personal Characteristics (Dealing with Others)

Able to compromise
Able to "to think on one's feet"—"wing it"
Accessible
Enabler and facilitator
Evenhanded
Exercises good judgment
Explains decisions
Flexibility
Inspires trust
Listens (actively)
Sense of humor
Treats people with dignity/respect

Knowledge Areas (Professional Issues)

Assessment and evaluation
   Measurement and evaluation methods (including service quality measurement and
      outcomes and accreditation assessment)
   Program assessment and evaluation
Bibliographic control/information-seeking behavior
   Collection development
   Information formats
   Scholarly communication
Community analysis
   Demographic changes in the community
   Economic changes in the community
   Major foreign language(s) of community
   Roles of state/local public officials
   User expectations/information needs
Consortia/partnerships
   Collaborative arrangements between/among multicampus and statewide settings
      and other institutions
Information technologies
   Current technology and information systems as they apply to libraries
   Emerging technological trends
   Information delivery systems
Legal/political context
   Intellectual freedom
   Intellectual property rights
   Other legal and public policy issues (relevant to public libraries)

Table 6.2
Regrouping of the Qualities Displayed in Table 6.1 (continued)

Knowledge Areas (Professional Issues) (continued)

Management
  Change management
  Current human resources administration/personnel administration
  Digital libraries, their management or planning (including for branches and
    remote campuses)
  Distance education
  Fiscal management
  Knowledge of all library operations
  Time management
  Project management
  Public relations
  Resource sharing
Planning
  Facilities (including remote storage, remodeling, and multi-use buildings), long-
    range, strategic, technology, collection development, security, personnel
    development, marketing, and fundraising
  Goals (educational, research, and service) of the parent institution
Resource development
  Fundraising
  Funds management
  Grant writing
Strategic directions
  Community's view of the library
  Distance education
  Functions of library boards and friends' groups
  Understands the complex environment in which the library functions
Teaching/learning role
  Information literacy
Trends/innovations
  Education, higher and other
  Libraries
  Publishing industry
  Teaching and learning theory
  Also trends related to demographics

NOTES

1. J. Richard Hackman, *Leading Teams: Setting the Stage for Great Performances* (Boston: Harvard Business School Press, 2002), 211.
2. See John Seidel, *The Ethnograph v5.0™: A User's Guide* (Thousand Oaks, Calif.: Scolari, 1998). This guide explains how the product translates text concepts into a map of the text that helps to identify interrelations and discrete categories.
3. To increase the validity of Figure 6.4 and Table 6.1, we shared them with some library directors and teachers of graduate-level management courses to see if they accepted the characterizations. In a couple of cases, we asked for them to place a quality in its proper place. Their suggestions are reflected in Table 6.2.
4. Catherine J. Matthews, "Becoming a Chief Librarian: An Analysis of Transition Stages in Academic Library Leadership," *Library Trends* 50 (spring 2002): 593.
5. Hackman, *Leading Teams,* ix.

7

---·•··•·---

LEADERSHIP ASSESSMENT

> Instituting a leadership-centered culture is the ultimate act of leadership.[1]

Chapters 3, 4, and 5 identified qualities relevant to directors of academic and public libraries. However, there is likely to be institutional variation in the relative importance of those qualities, and it is highly unlikely that any director will have gained mastery of an entire list, especially the one depicted in Table 3.1. Members of the senior management team who serve as assistant/associate/deputy librarians (AULs) may possess a set of qualities that complement the directors. Thus, the appointment of high-quality AULs is crucial for the successful management of the organization—enabling the library to meet its stated mission and to play a vital role within the parent institution.

Despite the fact that probably no director excels on every quality, readers will be interested in the comparisons made in chapter 6 and in the subsets of the qualities identified. Perhaps attention should focus on these subsets and not the entire list. Anyway, other than for personality traits and for a characterization of their intelligence, individuals do not merely possess a set of qualities. It is not a yes-or-no proposition; in other words, they possess qualities to varying extents. As a result, readers may want to explore the use of self-diagnostic tools to measure the extent to which they are proficient on a given set of qualities and to inform their personal development. They might also want others (i.e., their colleagues, directors, and other leaders they know and work with, and those conducting leadership institutes and mentoring programs) to appraise the extent of their mastery of any set of the qualities. This chapter assists in these efforts as well as reviewing some other uses for the qualities discussed in the previous chapters.

ASSESSMENT TOOLS

A number of psychometric assessment tools are designed to explore the extent to which those individuals completing an inventory possess leadership or managerial qualities. They also measure ability and personality. The scores obtained from these tools allow individuals to measure themselves against a much larger pool of respondents and to gain a general impression of their leadership or management capability. Still, each tool reflects a particular set of assumptions about leadership and management, and rarely does a single tool provide a direct measure of leadership or managerial performance; instead, tools probe an individual's perceptions of his or her performance. Because self-perceptions are subjective, test-makers need to validate the results by correlating scores with actual performance. If those individuals scoring high on a particular tool actually perform well on the job, that tool has value in predicting success. As is evident, an advantage of relying on a formal tool that has been used over time is that its reliability and validity have been tested and demonstrated. Still, leadership tests "do not adequately measure commitment. This characteristic will only manifest itself during training or crisis. Another problem with leadership tests is the psychological effects they have on the employee taking the test and those who do not."[2]

A search of U.S. national and state government resources on the portal FirstGov (http://www.firstgov.gov/) identifies more than 1,000 papers and inventories related to "managerial leadership assessment." Conducting a search of Google (http://www.google.com/) or another general search engine, using the terms "managerial assessment," "leadership assessment," and "managerial leadership assessment," reveals a variety of assessment tools. For example, InterLink Training and Coaching LLC, Anthem, Arizona, provides an online Leadership Assessment Tool, which consists of twenty-five questions for anyone to complete. The person can tally the points earned and receive general feedback on his or her leadership potential (see http://www.interlinktc.com/assessment.html).

The CCI Assessment Group developed the Leadership Assessment Survey, which is a 360-degree inventory "that focuses upon an individual's leadership skills and abilities" (http://www.pantesting.com/products/CCI/las.asp). The purpose of a 360-degree assessment is to provide participants with feedback on their approach to management of the workplace. In such assessments, supervisors, peers, customers, and other stakeholders provide the feedback. They complete the same tool or inventory as the participant did, and the results are compared to highlight someone's job-related strengths and to identify areas for further development.

The U.S. Office of Personnel Management offers another 360-degree program, which is "an intensive, five-day program designed to meet the needs of individuals who wish to move into leadership roles or who are in the initial phases of management careers" (http://www.leadership.opm.gov/content.cfm?cat=LAP). Students complete personnel assessment inventories,

personality/temperament profiles, and a case study analysis, and they participate in various problem-solving activities. Multirater feedback (360-degree
feedback) includes feedback from assessment professionals and opportunities
for self-observation (via videotaped sessions); such practices are integral
aspects of the program.

Leadership/Impact® (*L/I*), available from Human Synergistics/Center for
Applied Research, Inc., is a copyrighted inventory that "provides managers
and executives with unique insights into their leadership strategies and the
impact of those strategies on the behavior and performance of others"
(http://www.hscar.co/li.htm). Team Management Services (TMS)
(http://www.tms.co.nz/instruments.htm) provides instruments such as the
Team Management Index (TMI) that addresses leadership, team building,
and other areas.

The Center for Creative Leadership (CCL*), founded in North Carolina
in 1970 by the South Richardson Foundation Inc., "is a nonprofit educational institution devoted to behavioral science research and leadership education." Today, CCL has locations in Colorado, California, and Belgium, and
it "maintains relationships with more than 20 Network Associates and other
partners in the United States and abroad."[3] CCL offers fee-based assessment
tools, each aimed at different audiences in the global economy. For example,
one instrument, called 360 by Design SM, enables "the client" (e.g., an organization using it) to select from among seventy competencies grouped by
"thematic areas for purposes of clarity and organization only" (see
http://www.ccl.org/products/360bd/competencies.htm).

The Campbell Interest and Skills Survey (CISS), provided by NCS Assessments, "measures self-reported vocational interests and skills." It also "goes
beyond traditional inventories by adding parallel skill scales that provide estimates of an individual's confidence in his or her ability to perform various
occupational activities" (see http://assessments.ncs.com/assessments/
tests/ciss.htm).

R. E. Brown Company and Associates has a shareware offer: "If you find
this assessment helpful [for management/leadership], please send us $10 for
each employee who completes the form and receives the report." The survey
consists of forty questions, half related to management and half to leadership.
Respondents calculate their response totals and can review their answers
for "any surprises or challenges" (see http://rebrown.com/rebrown/
orascale.htm; also see http://www.rebrown.com/rebrown/leadch2.htm).

A "Leadership Self-Assessment" is available at http://www.nsba.org/
sbot/toolkit/LeadSA.html. The Web site provides a list of attributes, skills,
and knowledge areas and then itemizes tools for improved advocacy;
improved inquiry; individual self-assessment when you are at an impasse; and
leadership behavior.

Assessment Systems Corporation (http://www.assess.com/panbypub.
htm) highlights a number of publishers and their products (i.e., tests and sur-

veys). More detailed information, including the cost of using an instrument, is available. The Buros Institute (http://www.unl.edu/buros/index18. html) also provides access to numerous tests.

Another option is to rely on the critically acclaimed *Mental Measurements Yearbook* (Highland Park, N.J.: Mental Measurements Yearbook, 1941–) and select inventories that might be applicable locally. Tests such as the "Profile of Aptitude for Leadership" (Training-House, Inc., 1991), which measures an individual's relative strength in each of four leadership styles (or types of leader), requires payment of a fee for its administration and interpretation. The *Mental Measurements Yearbook* contains critical reviews of each inventory provided as well as identifying the population that might be studied (e.g., adults) and whether it is administered to groups and/or individuals.

Leadership That Works has developed an inventory, Coaching Skills Assessment, which it sells for $10.00 (570-297-2270) (see http://www. leadershipthaworks.com/Coaching/C05CoachingAssessment.htm). Typically, coaching and leadership inventories provide a set of questions on which participants rate themselves, perhaps using a five-point scale. Once they answer the questions, they total the number of points earned and see where they fall within a range of scores that interpret the results.

A rather unorthodox approach to assessing leadership potential is the use of biographical measures of personality traits. In a study published in 1998, Lawrence J. Stricker and Donald A. Rock attempted "to demonstrate the feasibility of biographical inventories free of the limitations common to many current biographical measures by constructing and validating an inventory composed of homogeneous scales, with item content that is factual and fair, to assess personality traits predictive of leadership."[4] The researchers developed scales for dominance, emotional stability, need for achievement, self-confidence, and sociability. In their study of midshipmen at the U.S. Naval Academy, they found that all of the scales, except self-confidence, correlated with leadership criteria based on peer ratings of leadership traits, military performance grades, and promotion after graduating and serving as an officer.

A first step for anyone interested in management and leadership might be to take the Myers-Briggs Type Indicator® (MBTI), an instrument provided by Consulting Psychologists Press, Inc. (http://www.cpp-db.com/ products/mbti/index.asp), which measures a person's preferences, using four scales with opposite poles: (1) extraversion to introversion, (2) sensing to intuition, (3) thinking to feeling, and (4) judging to perceiving. The combination of these preferences results in sixteen distinct personality types and insights into a person's way of communication.[5]

The Blake and Mouton Managerial Grid (see, for instance, http://www.nwlink.com/~donclark/leader/bm_model.html) is one of the more frequently used inventories to measure leadership behavior and the type of leadership style that participants demonstrate (e.g., "team leader" and "authoritarian leader"). A cautionary note is provided: "like any other instrument that attempts to profile a person, you have to take in other factors, such as how do your manager and employees rate you as a leader, do you get your job done, do you take care of your employees, are you GROWING [*sic*] your organization, etc."

Instead of (or in addition to) taking one of these tests, it might be useful to create a new instrument (see the section on "self-diagnostic tools"). Finally, for fun, one might complete a skills quiz that compares twentieth-century leaders to twenty-first-century leaders and shows the new leader is more skilled in communicating in different forms (e.g., in person and electronically).[6]

ASSESSMENT OF LIBRARY DIRECTORS

In an article published in 2001, James F. Williams II "explores the topic of leadership assessment through a review of the literature, a review of the counterbalancing arguments on the topic of performance reviews, and an exploration of the societal and institutional context within which these reviews take place in academia."[7] He also briefly considers the library leader's portfolio and a process by which to assess the performance of library leaders. Williams lists the following items that he believes should be considered in the assessment of a university library director:

Leadership

- Strategic vision and goals for the library organization;
- Campuswide role and contributions;
- Initiative and creativity;
- Efforts to build community, maintain morale, inspire others; and
- Other.

Academic Planning

- Instructional mission of the library organization;
- Research/creative work mission of the library organization; and
- Understanding of how the library organization's mission/functions relate to that of other units, and of the campus as a whole.

Management and Decision Making

- Effective use and fair allocation of resources (financial, space, time, personnel, equipment, physical, and virtual information resources);
- Timely decisions and consistent follow-up on decisions;
- Management of disputes;

- Effective use of personnel;
- Delegation of authority;
- Deserved recognition of others;
- Setting reasonable standards and expectations;
- Consultation and consensus building;
- Investing time and energy for high-quality performance; and
- Other.

Diversity

- Commitment and record.

External Relations

- Representation to external constituents;
- Friend-raising;
- Fundraising; and
- Other.

Communication

- Effective listening; and
- Effective communication with, and has support of, librarians, staff, faculty, students, other administrators, and external constituencies.

Professional Development

- Informed of developments in the profession of research librarianship, and in higher education generally;
- Retains currency in the profession of research librarianship through scholarship, instruction, and/or professional activities;
- Mentoring leadership development; and
- Other.[8]

Williams concludes with the statement that "an essential ingredient for success in the library organization is an assessment process that monitors and promotes effective leadership."[9] He argues that such a process works best when it is formal; contains documented process guidelines and criteria specific to the leadership position under review; is conducted on the basis of clear goals and jointly developed performance expectations; utilizes multi-source feedback mechanisms; and is cognizant of the distinct societal and institutional context within which the library leader is being reviewed.[10]

One of the first formal assessments of management skills and leadership qualities in librarianship took place from 1979 to 1983 at the Career Development and Assessment Center for Librarians (CDACL).[11] In an article, Peter Hiatt explains how assessment technology identifies and improves leadership and management skills and how assessment centers can identify and nurture leadership in library and information studies. He defines an assessment center as "a comprehensive standardized procedure in which multiple assessment techniques, such as situational exercises and job simulations (e.g., games, discussion groups, in-basket exercises, reports, and presentations) are used to evaluate individual employees."[12]

The CDACL emphasized the principles of networking and effective professional and association involvement. The typical assessment center procedure involved a day devoted to orientation for the learners, one-on-one interviews, and group discussions. During a second day, those learners made oral presentations related to their case studies and participated in simulation exercises. On a third day, the learners and a director conducted one-on-one interviews regarding the competency profiles that had emerged from the previous assessment processes.[13]

The CDACL evaluated participants on fourteen management dimensions grouped into two broad categories: communication and management. Communication includes listening, oral communication, sensitivity, and written communication skills; whereas management focuses on decisiveness, delegation, flexibility, initiative, judgment (decision making), leadership, management control, planning and organizing, problem analysis/solving, and tolerance for stress.[14] Participants' scores on these fourteen dimensions were used to develop management profiles that could be used for self-assessment, the design of staff development and continuing education activities, and so on.

In 1997, the American Library Trustee Association of the American Library Association published a pamphlet on how to evaluate directors of public libraries. A survey was conducted to "find out if public library directors are evaluated regularly, what types of evaluations are used, what criteria have been established for evaluation, and which persons or group performs the evaluation."[15] Fifty-eight percent of the respondents reported that their library director was evaluated, and 76 percent of those evaluated the director every year. Seventy percent of the respondents who evaluated the director employed a structured format, 14 percent used a written report from the director, and 12 percent had a meeting to discuss the director's performance. The most commonly used evaluation criteria were:

- Completion of goals and/or objectives;
- Comparison of job performance with job description;
- Factor comparison of qualities such as knowledge and communication skills;
- Departmental operation in all areas;
- Comparison with individual expectations;
- Behaviors;

- Overall opinion of each board member;
- Effective representation of the library; and
- Activities and training.

In 65 percent of the responding libraries, the public library board or board chairperson completed the evaluation. For 30 percent of the responding libraries, a city official completed the process. The pamphlet includes fourteen sample evaluation forms.

Two documents about evaluation of academic library directors have been published in the past few years. "OLMS Occasional Paper 21," produced by ARL's Office of Leadership and Management Services, presents the results of a study of current practice and a checklist of recommendations. It identifies eleven external and internal university library director leadership roles that can be used in developing evaluation criteria. The external roles are (1) chief representative and spokesperson; (2) campus administrator; (3) liaison; (4) monitor; (5) negotiator and advocate; and (6) fundraiser. The internal roles focus on: (1) leader of planning and operations; (2) leader of staff; (3) communicator; (4) change agent and entrepreneur; and (5) resource allocator.[16]

The other document, ARL SPEC Kit 229, presents the results of a survey on the executive review process for ARL directors, provides several representative documents, and concludes with a checklist of recommendations.[17] Sixty-nine percent of the responding directors reported having some sort of formal performance review; in 59 percent of the institutions the provost initiated the review; 41 percent responded that the review guidelines were formally established and documented; and most of the respondents indicated that they were generally satisfied with the review process. An abridged version of the checklist of recommendations includes the following:

Review Process Guidelines

- Availability of a formal review process;
- Availability of documented procedural guidelines for the review;
- Existence of a clear purpose for the review;
- Satisfactory frequency of review;
- Specific, candid feedback;
- Discussions of institutional and library priorities, goals, and objectives; and
- Opportunity for director to provide documentation or context.

Review Process Criteria

- Availability of documented, specific criteria;
- Measurement of director's success in achieving negotiated expectations;
- Adequate recognition of changing and evolving roles of director; and
- Adequate distinction between performance of library and of director.

Review Process Participants

- Opportunity for a variety of participants;
- Adequate weight given to those who know director's performance firsthand;
- Involvement of a peer administrator; and
- Active involvement of the director's supervisor.[18]

One might complete one of the other assessment tools discussed in this section of the chapter or in the appendices of Rosie L. Albritton and Thomas W. Shaughnessy's *Developing Leadership Skills*,[19] assuming that the individual is interested in being a manager and leader of an academic or public library.

SELF-DIAGNOSTIC TOOLS

The figures and tables in chapters 3 through 6 that depict qualities could be converted into self-diagnostic tools. For any of those lists, respondents might rate the extent to which they have met each quality identified. For an example, Table 7.1 adopts qualities from the category of "leading" in Table 3.1.

As an alternative to the scale used in Table 7.1, they might rate themselves on a four-point scale, with

1 = Seldom   2 = Occasionally   3 = Frequently   4 = Always

Or, on a five-point scale, with

Seldom   Always
1   2   3   4   5

Table 7.1
Self-Diagnostic Tools

Fall short of the quality			Exactly meet the quality		Exceed the quality (have exceptional ability/skills)	
−3	−2	−1	0	+1	+2	+3
• I function well in a political environment	−3	−2	−1	0	+1	+2	+3
• I develop a campus visibility for the library	−3	−2	−1	0	+1	+2	+3
• I am an advocate for librarians' role in higher education	−3	−2	−1	0	+1	+2	+3
• I think "outside the box" (in new and creative ways applicable to the problem)	−3	−2	−1	0	+1	+2	+3

MOVING BEYOND SELF-ASSESSMENT

Frederick C. Wendel, Allan H. Schmidt, and James Loch note that paper-and-pencil tests provide indicators or signs, rather than samples, of leadership capability (just as passing a written driver's test does not guarantee the ability to handle a car effectively).[20] To simulate 360-degree assessment, it is important that others who participate in the assessment process help to minimize the bias or extent of exaggeration of self-ratings. To increase the learning opportunity and to generate valuable feedback, these other individuals could comment on all scores less than the ideal ("+3," "+4," or "+5," depending on the scale used). They might also offer examples of instances in which a given quality was demonstrated or lacking. The purpose is to include instances of real behavior in the assessment.

Questionnaires and comments from peers or individuals to whom one reports need not be the only methods of assessment. Respondents might also prepare portfolios (collected examples of their work over time) and identify those qualities met (and under what circumstances). Since leadership institutes tend to focus on case studies, those analyses and any written comments provided might be added to the portfolio. Again, individuals might ask others to review and comment on the collected work.

Another technique is to maintain a journal or diary in which daily problems and their solutions are identified. Most importantly, those qualities met (and unmet) should be discussed with others, perhaps at brown bag lunches, at special meetings held at professional associations, or in more private surroundings (one-to-one). Individuals might also request that their performance evaluation include a set of qualities (the amount listed—as well as the specific ones—might be negotiated) and that the evaluation then focuses on the extent of their accomplishment. Finally, 360-degree assessment reminds us that the perspectives of customers and other stakeholders merit representation as long as they are in a position to provide meaningful insights.

OTHER USES OF THE QUALITIES

It is conceivable that anyone pursuing a directorship of an academic or public library might identify those qualities that he or she regards as strengths and list them in a cover letter in the application for a position, as well as in the accompanying curriculum vitae. At the same time, during an interview with a search team or a headhunting firm that oversees the selection process, specific qualities might be discussed and probed. Those individuals called on to support an individual's candidacy for a position might also respond to queries about that person's strengths and weaknesses regarding leadership and managerial qualities. Naturally, any discussion should not treat qualities in isolation of other factors (e.g., leadership styles, which qualities the director must possess, and which ones the management team might have). Nonetheless, the director will be expected to play a leadership role in the larger community and, more than likely, must demonstrate his or her mastery of those qualities. Key qualities might relate to dealing with the external environment and serving as a team leader. As J. Richard Hackman, a professor of social and organizational psychology at Harvard University, explains, "anyone and everyone who clarifies a team's direction, or improves its structure, or secures organizational support for it, or provides coaching that improves its performance processes is providing team leadership....So long as the focus of leadership activities is on creating conditions that enhance team performance, the more leadership the better."[21]

Another technique centers on the use of a report card, where the director has "an opportunity to identify those areas in which he or she is presumed to be performing and for which they seek feedback."[22] Adopting from this technique, senior staff might ask department heads and others serving under them for a critical appraisal of their collegiality, attitudes, and performance. Naturally, anyone seeking the appraisal must be willing to accept constructive criticism, and they should not penalize staff for their frank appraisal. Conceivably, some people outside the library, but within the organization, might participate. Some of the qualities identified in this book might even be added to the so-called report card.

"Keeping a work journal," declares Katherine Murphy Dickson, who is retired from Caroline County Public Library (in Denton, Maryland), "can be useful in exploring one's thoughts and feelings about work challenges and work decisions." She discusses the journal and offers advice about how long to maintain it and what to include in it. The diarist and others could review the written work and reflect on what is written. For instance, the writing will reveal "the role work plays in your life."[23] Given the commitment of the director to the position, such insights are worthy of note.

CONCLUSION

There are a number of choices that readers have to diagnose their leadership styles and capabilities, as we all wonder, "How do we describe, understand and predict the behaviour of individuals in organizations? This...question has intrigued academicians and practitioners of organizational science alike for decades, despite the fact that we already know the answer—that is, it depends on a certain set of conditions and interactions among variables."[24] Related questions are "How do we recognize which qualities have the most value on an institutional basis?" and "How can we best prepare individuals to gain competency with those qualities?'" Researchers Allan H. Church and Janine Waclawski answer the first related question,[25] and the next chapter also addresses the other related question and discusses the acquisition of the qualities.

The qualities presented in this book focus on librarianship and the types of directors needed for the near future. Those qualities were developed with input from a number of directors and other members of the senior management team. Thus, the lists presented in chapters 3 through 5 were developed with directors of academic and public libraries in mind. Commentaries in these chapters also attempt to identify the more prized qualities; chapter 6 helps in this regard. Thus, it might be useful for others to continue to convert the qualities identified in the previous chapter into inventories that might be linked to leadership styles and that present case studies useful for analysis and role playing. Further testing might also lead to an interpretative scoring of one's performance on any self-diagnostic inventories that emerge. At the same time, to be most useful, those inventories should be converted into 360-degree assessments so that the perspectives of multiple groups are represented.

> One way to develop leadership is to create challenging opportunities for young employees.[26]

> Leadership complements management; it doesn't replace it.[27]

NOTES

1. John P. Kotter, *John P. Kotter on What Leaders Really Do* (Boston: Harvard Business School Press, 1999), 65.
2. See Christopher Rowe, "Picking the Winners: The Thorny Issue of Assessing Leadership Potential," *Leadership and Organization Development Journal* 15 (October 1994): S1–S5.
3. Center for Creative Leadership, *Assessment Tools and Performance Support at a Glance* (Greensboro, N.C.: Center for Creative Leadership, n.d.) (available: http://www.ccl.org/assessments).
4. Lawrence J. Stricker and Donald A. Rock, "Assessing Leadership Potential with a Biographical Measure of Personality Traits," *International Journal of Selection and Assessment* 6 (1998): 164.
5. See William L. Gardner and Mark J. Martinko, "Using the Myers-Briggs Type Indicator to Study Managers: A Literature Review and Research Agenda," *Journal of Management* 22 (spring 1996): 45–84. See also Bonnie G. Mani, "Progress on the Journey to Total Quality Management: Using the Myers-Briggs Type Indicator and the Adjective Check List in Management Development," *Public Personnel Management* 24 (fall 1995): 365–401.
6. Richard G. Ensman Jr., "Twenty-First Century Skills Quiz," *Doors and Hardware* 61 (November 1997): 60–64.
7. James F. Williams II, "Leadership Evaluation and Assessment," *Journal of Library Administration*™ 32, nos. 3–4 (2001): 145.
8. Ibid., 162–63.
9. Ibid., 164.
10. Ibid.
11. Peter Hiatt, Ruth H. Hamilton, and Charlotte Wood, *Assessment Centers for Professional Library Leadership: A Report to the Profession from the Career Development and Assessment Center for Librarians* (Chicago: American Library Association, 1993). This book describes this assessment.

12. Peter Hiatt, "Identifying and Encouraging Leadership Potential: Assessment Technology and the Library Profession," *Library Trends* 40 (1992): 514.

13. Ibid., 517.

14. Ibid., 520–24.

15. Sharon A. Saulman, ed., *Sample Evaluations of Library Directors* (Chicago: American Library Association, American Library Trustee Association, 1997), 2.

16. George J. Soete, *Evaluating Library Directors: A Study of Current Practice and a Checklist of Recommendations,* OLMS Occasional Paper, no. 21 (Washington, D.C.: Association of Research Libraries, Office of Leadership and Management Services, May 1998), 36–38.

17. George J. Soete, *Evaluating Academic Library Directors,* SPEC Kit 229 (Washington, D.C.: Association of Research Libraries, Office of Leadership and Management Services, May 1998).

18. Ibid., 87–88.

19. Rosie L. Albritton and Thomas W. Shaughnessy, eds., *Developing Leadership Skills: A Source Book for Librarians* (Englewood, Col.: Libraries Unlimited, 1990). Appendices reprint inventories for measuring one's leadership potential, transformational management skills, interpersonal communication skills, ability to handle stress, stress pattern, decision making, understanding conflict, and assertiveness. There is also a Quality-of-Life Index.

20. Frederick C. Wendel, Allan H. Schmidt, and James Loch, "Measurements of Personality and Leadership: Some Relationships" (Lincoln, Nebr.: University of Nebraska, 1992) (ED 350 694).

21. J. Richard Hackman, *Leading Teams: Setting the Stage for Great Performances* (Boston: Harvard Business School Press, 2002), 211.

22. Catherine J. Matthews, "Becoming a Chief Librarian: An Analysis of Transition Stages in Academic Library Leadership," *Library Trends* 50 (spring 2002): 595. The appendix (597–600) reprints the report card.

23. Katherine Murphy Dickson, "A Work Journal," *Library Trends* 50 (spring 2002): 687, 700–701.

24. Allan H. Church and Janine Waclawski, "The Relationship between Individual Orientation and Executive Leadership Behaviour," *Journal of Occupational and Organizational Psychology* 71 (June 1998): 99.

25. Ibid.

26. Kotter, *John P. Kotter on What Leaders Really Do,* 63.

27. Ibid., 52.

8

—•═•—

ACQUIRING THE QUALITIES

> Leadership is not the work of some steely-eyed CEO, sitting in isolation
> and issuing ex-cathedra pronouncements.[1]

This chapter discusses different methods to acquire the qualities identified in
previous chapters (chapters 3 through 6). The first section discusses these
methods in general terms, while the second section relates the views of different leaders in the profession about which methods they consider, in general, the best for addressing particular qualities. A third section examines
leadership development programs more closely by reporting what some
states are doing. Figure 8.1, which highlights a hypothetical doctoral program in managerial leadership, indicates that any method could (or perhaps
should) identify those qualities that a proposed student must acquire. Then,
outcomes assessment could be applied to demonstrate the extent to which
those methods accomplish their stated purpose: changing the behavior, critical thinking, problem-solving ability, knowledge, and skill set of those participating in that method.

The choices presented in this chapter are not intended to be comprehensive or to address the offerings of specific programs; rather, the purpose is to
highlight some of the choices, especially those mentioned by survey respondents. Professional associations and programs of library and information
studies (LIS), for instance, may also offer continuing educational opportunities and workshops, and some LIS courses deal with leadership traits and
skills. Whatever program an individual selects ought to document expected
outcomes and provide outcomes assessment to examine program success or
effectiveness in response to a mission statement, goals, and objectives. As
noted subsequently, not all of the qualities can be learned. Some result from

Figure 8.1
Hypothetical Doctoral Program (Managerial Leadership)

MISSION/GOALS

The program offers advanced study in preparation for managerial leadership and focuses on the knowledge, skills, competencies, and personal traits applicable to leadership in libraries, other nonprofit organizations, and other information-intensive enterprises. The increasing need for such a program arises from the expanding complexity of organizations and the need for educating leaders in rapidly changing organizations in which knowledge and intellectual capital are critical for success.

The cohesive program concentrates on: (1) a comprehensive understanding of diverse issues and a strong foundation in critical thinking; problem solving; practice-based research; and effective writing, learning, and oral presentation; (2) interactivity using technology; and (3) students able to explore their potential in a supportive, nurturing environment of individualized study that combines technological applications, research methods, change, and political realities with management and leadership theory and practice.

Management is an applied discipline that requires both academic preparation and substantial experience. The goals of the program therefore are to:

- Prepare individuals for a career as change agents and leaders in managing libraries, media centers, nonprofit organizations, and other information-related organizations in an environment of globalization and of a convergence of disciplines;
- Create a learning environment in which inquiry and raising questions are valued and individual strengths are enhanced;
- Engender in students an ability to engage in critical thinking and problem solving;
- Establish a culture that nurtures the advancement and dissemination of new knowledge related to managing libraries as complex organizations;
- Provide students with a conceptual understanding of organizations and behavior within them;
- Develop competencies in interpersonal and communication skills, leadership, and facilitation; and
- Develop an understanding of the role of technology in the management of change.

POTENTIAL AUDIENCE

The program caters to those individuals who are already employed in full-time positions and do not want to leave their positions to earn a degree. Thus, courses would be offered each fall, spring, and summer, and classes would be offered on weekends. Target groups include:

- Department heads to associate/assistant/deputy directors in libraries in the Association of Research Libraries (ARL);
- Department heads to directors in libraries in the Association of College and Research Libraries (ACRL); and
- Department heads to directors in large urban public libraries

APPLICATION

As part of the application process, prospective students will submit an essay addressing their level of attainment of the following abilities:

Oral and written communication	Leadership
Critical thinking	Innovation
Listening and memory	Humor (as part of leadership)
Motivating others	

From the above list of qualities, the applicant will be asked to prepare and deliver a thirty-minute presentation to the Doctoral Committee.

THE PROGRAM OF STUDY

Students are expected to exhibit steady progress on a number of key areas:

- Domain knowledge;
- Analysis/critical thinking;
- Engagement in research and scholarship; and
- Presentation/communication skills.

Required Components (Tentative)

Contemporary Leadership Theory; Contemporary Management, Research as a Managerial Activity; Evaluation of Library Services (containing components on Systems Analysis and Statistics); Issues in Leadership and Change (the capstone course, which is taken before the comprehensive examination); and the Management Research Study (MRS), the culminating research project that is focused on the area of managerial leadership.

Required Projects

Prior to the capstone course, students will take an independent study in which they develop, execute, and report on a small-scale study that is capable of publication. Furthermore, prior to the comprehensive examination, students will complete the Issue Analysis: interview four directors with expertise in their area of interest (e.g., ACRL libraries) and write an analysis of two of those issues drawing on the related literature.

Possible Elective Courses

Project Management; Strategic Planning and Organizational Change; Digital Libraries; Social Informatics; Managing in a Political Context (Power Structures and Influencing a Culture); Managing Teams; and Human Resources Management. There might be *Special Topics* , examples of which are:

Fundraising (development of a capital campaign planning document); Legal Issues; Trends in Higher Education; Ethical Considerations in Management; Managing the Challenges of Diversity; Conflict Resolution; Library Architecture and Design; Financial Management in Public Sector Organizations; Information Policy; Mobilization for Political Action; Personnel Management; Interactive Leadership; and Facilitation.

ATTRIBUTES GAINED THROUGH THE PROGRAM

Upon completion of the program, students will have gained mastery of the following set of attributes:

Administrative Skills
- Able to analyze and solve problems, able to demonstrate organizational agility, able to demonstrate team-building skills, able to manage fiscal resources/budgets, able to ask the right questions

Communication Skills
- Able to communicate effectively with staff/public (good interpersonal/people skills), articulate (good oral/written/presentation skills), able to "think on one's feet"—"wing it"

Creativity

Figure 8.1
Hypothetical Doctoral Program (Managerial Leadership) (continued)

- Able to think "outside the box" (in new and creative ways applicable to the problem)

Information Technology
- Able to plan for life cycles of information technologies

Knowledge Base
- Broad knowledge of issues (scholarly communication, financial management, planning, digital libraries, information technology, collection management and development, outcomes assessment, user expectations/information needs, intellectual property rights, fundraising, public relations, service quality measurement, goal setting, information delivery systems, publishing industry, and security of property and individuals)

Leadership
- Able to articulate direction for the library, able to function in a political environment, able to manage/shape change as well as the library's culture, able to create an environment that fosters accountability, shows reasonable risk-taking skills, able to develop various sources of funds (e.g., grants, gifts)

Applicable Cognate Areas (e.g., Library Knowledge)
- Able to anticipate the needs of various constituencies, able to create and implement systems that enhance the value of the library to its public and stakeholders, service orientation

Personal Qualities
- Able to treat people with dignity and respect, able to be diplomatic, a good listener, a good facilitator, open-minded, able to work effectively in groups (as appropriate), persuasive, able to establish priorities, committed to a set of values (integrity), sense of humor, able to take initiative, self-awareness of strengths and weaknesses, sense of perspective, commitment to service

CENTER ON MANAGERIAL LEADERSHIP

The Center would include a Professor of Practice (*a very well known individual from industry, higher education, or communication—someone who is at the top of his/her profession—who, for a period of time, might teach before going to another career position; this person will bring practical experience and a national/international reputation to the classroom and program*). The Center will provide a place for students to receive support, including mentoring; continue their development; and share ongoing research. All students working on the Management Research Paper and the MRS would be affiliated with the Center. The Professor of Practice will be involved in a series of leadership institutes related to the program of study (those institutes may attract individuals outside the doctoral program—to compete with other leadership institutes). The Center would perform consulting services for those libraries with which it enters a partnership relationship. These services might focus on managerial research studies conducted in cooperation with those libraries.

a person's upbringing, some are traits that people are born with, some emerge from a nurturing workplace, and others are formally learned. This chapter indicates which qualities survey respondents suspected are internal to the person. In some instances, formal programs might enhance or further develop one's inherent qualities.

GENERAL WAYS TO ACQUIRE THE QUALITIES

This section does not endorse any particular method. Rather, the intent is to provide a general overview of various choices. Undoubtedly, some programs are very effective and provide a solid foundation, but individuals are probably most successful when they pursue diverse options as they develop their pool of knowledge and experiences related to management and leadership.

Leadership Development Programs

A number of leadership programs and institutes exist at the national and state levels. The Association of Research Libraries' Office of Leadership and Management Services (ARL/OLMS), for example, focuses on leadership development. It offers "information and services designed to build and strengthen the professional expertise and leadership skills of librarians who face the challenges of today's library while anticipating tomorrow's advances."[2] The Office of Leadership and Management Services provides workshops, educational programs (via an online lyceum), a diversity program, and more.

Examples of leadership institutes include the Senior Fellows program at the University of California, Los Angeles; the Association of College and Research Libraries (ACRL)/Harvard Leadership Institute; the Snowbird Leadership Institute;[3] Northern Exposure to Leadership;[4] the Frye Institute; and the Executive Leadership Institute of the Urban Libraries Council. A program of the Council on Library and Information Resources, EDUCAUSE, and Emory University, the Frye Institute is an intensive, two-week-long, residential program held at Emory University in Atlanta, Georgia. Participants, who are selected competitively from a group of applicants and nominees, "study and analyze leadership challenges stemming from the changing context and complexity of higher education. The program will pay special attention to the implications of the growing power of information technology to transform the means of research, teaching and scholarly communication." Upon completion of the residential portion of the institute, participants "conduct a year-long practicum, to explore, within their own institutional environment, the issues and questions raised during the institute."[5] As a result, the Frye Institute provides more than episodic coverage of leadership; it also seeks a more sustained commitment to learning.

The Urban Libraries Council's Executive Leadership Institute, which is aimed at public librarianship, seeks to prepare "a new generation of leaders." It includes seminars "that focus on individual, institutional and community leadership, change, politics and strategy"; real-time leadership challenges "chosen by each library team to address throughout the Institute"; and ongoing coaching support, "during which expert coaches will work with each team to develop, implement and evaluate their work on their chosen Leadership Challenge."[6]

Mentoring

As Gordon F. Shea notes, mentoring is "a developmental, caring, sharing, and helping relationship where one person [mentor] invests time, know-how, and effort in enhancing another person's [mentee's/protégé's] growth, knowledge, and skills, and responds to critical needs in the life of that person in ways that prepare the individual for greater productivity or achievement in the future."[7] Mentoring occurs on an informal or formal basis, locally or on a larger scale, and it requires a mentee to formulate goals and objectives with which the mentor agrees. These goals and objectives need to match institutional goals as well.

A library director and other members of the senior management team might formally mentor selected subordinates whom they identified as likely to progress as managers and leaders in the library and perhaps even in the profession. Mentoring also occurs, for instance, as librarians seek promotion and tenure, and receive guidance in meeting the institution's research expectations related to their annual performance. Mentoring has benefits for the mentor, mentee, and the institution to which the mentee is affiliated. "Benefits to the mentee . . . [include] receiving tenure, emotional support, input from more than a supervisor, making friends and gaining confidence more quickly, having a relationship with an experienced librarian, getting quickly on track for tenure and promotion, and receiving more information early on about the library and the university." For the mentor, the benefits include "the chance to offer support, satisfaction for contributing to the growth of staff, and learning from new ideas and perspectives."[8] For the institution, the benefits relate to the likely retention of good staff and the application of the insights gained to the resolution of local problems.[9]

One of the best-known formal efforts is the College Library Directors Mentor Program,[10] which emerged in the early 1990s to meet the perceived "need to enhance leadership capabilities of new college library directors and to help them meet the challenges involved in directing libraries in small colleges. This program meets this need by fostering a mentoring relationship with an experienced library director."[11]

Another program is the National Library of Medicine/Association of Academic Health Science Libraries Leadership Fellows Program, which is designed to "introduce academic health sciences library managers to leadership theory and practical tools for implementing change at organizational and professional levels"; "develop meaningful professional relationships between fellows and current directors, through mentoring partnerships"; "expose fellows to another academic health sciences library under the guidance of their mentors"; and "create a cohort of learners who will draw upon each other for support throughout their careers."[12]

Formal Programs of Study

Some directors of academic and other types of libraries have a degree(s) in addition to (or, in some instances, in place of) a master's degree in LIS from a program accredited by the American Library Association. For example, they might have a second master's degree, such as in business administration, or a Ph.D. degree, which is a research degree not aimed exclusively or largely at management or leadership. A Ph.D. program specializing in managerial leadership in the information professions would have a clear market niche, but, to date, has not yet been introduced by any LIS school. Such a program could involve partnerships with professional associations and universities, as students pursue studies in managerial leadership, while receiving formal training in the conduct of research useful to the progressive management of academic, public, and other types of libraries and public sector organizations. Neither leadership institutes nor mentoring can offer the same type of formal training in research that such a program could offer (see Figure 8.1). Research develops one's capacity for problem solving and critical thinking as well as including both evaluation and assessment.

OUTCOMES ASSESSMENT

The types of techniques discussed in chapter 7 could be used in conjunction with leadership institutes and mentoring to ask individuals participating in learning programs to compile a record of their professional and learning development over time. Equally as important, educational programs, leadership institutes, and formal mentoring programs could identify those qualities depicted in chapters 3 through 6 in which participants want to specialize, and then they could use outcomes assessment to determine the extent to which they acquired the particular sets of qualities. For example, Figure 8.1 claims that such a hypothetical doctoral program results in the accomplishment of qualities related to administrative skills, communication skills, creativity, information technology, leadership, library knowledge, and a basic set of knowledge. It also covers some personal qualities. Two questions are

1. How well have those claims been met?
2. What type of documentation does the program offer as proof of their attainment?

In general, learning outcomes are concerned with those attributes and abilities, both cognitive and affective, that reflect the knowledge that learners gained from the educational experience. More precisely, one may ask, "What do they know that they did not know before?" and "What can they do that they could not do before?" These questions focus on program credibility and accountability. Outcomes assessment draws on direct and indirect measures of learning. Indirect measures are sources of assessment data that, when used to supplement direct measures, provide information that may enrich or illuminate aspects of what the direct measures suggest about learning. These measures ascertain the *perceived* extent or value of learning experiences, and they include surveys, follow-up studies (e.g., retention rates and completion rates), exit interviews, employment trends, and job placement data. On the other hand, direct measures of learning are performance based, focusing on the actual work that learners produced.

One direct method that is relevant to this chapter is the developmental portfolio, which represents collected samples of learners' work over time (e.g., the length of the mentoring program or the leadership institute). Increasingly, there is a trend to use electronic portfolios. Portfolios are linked to publicly stated goals and objectives related to learning; they document the participant's learning and development; they contain a clearly stated rationale for their use and program expectations for the learner to demonstrate; participants are given an opportunity to reflect on their learning as a consequence of selecting examples of the work they believe will document their attainment of each of the stated outcomes; and the findings from portfolio review are useful for making program changes to improve teaching and participant learning.

Perhaps, upon completion of a program, participants might develop a portfolio that can be subsequently reviewed. In some instances, mentoring programs and leadership institutes have a yearlong follow up to a short-term program; the purpose of the follow up is to reflect on and apply the insights gained under some type of individual instruction and guidance. Such circumstances lend themselves to portfolio review. Key factors to include are (1) assure that the sample of documents is representative; (2) develop appropriate protocols to deal with such procedures as the selection and consistency of the artifacts that are placed in the portfolio; (3) develop a reliable instrument and rating rubric to score the artifacts; and (4) train cross-disciplinary faculty evaluators to reduce the likelihood of low interrater reliability among judges.[13]

LEADERS' ASSESSMENT OF ACQUIRING THE QUALITIES

The authors identified a group of thirty leaders in academic and public librarianship who are well-known academic and public library directors, who serve in professional associations or who are state librarians, and who lead organizations that fund library development. We sent a survey to each leader that was based on one or more of the tables in chapters 3 through 5 that identified the qualities important to a type of library, and we asked them to rate, on a five-point scale, how that quality might best be acquired. The scale ranged from "minimally" (one) to "entirely" (five). The choices included "work experience," "mentoring," "leadership institute," and "other." We asked for a clarification of any response placed in the other category, including a formal degree program. Furthermore, if they did not see an option as viable, they were asked to leave that category blank.

Eighteen leaders (60 percent) agreed to participate in the study. Of them, six had expertise with ARL libraries, seven with other academic libraries, and five with public libraries. For this exploratory research, we felt that the small number of responses was sufficient to provide insights into the options and to the creation of additional groupings of the qualities for both academic and public libraries. Naturally, the rating of a particular option would likely vary if the number of respondents was increased.

Several respondents referred to an individual's character, belief and value system, upbringing, and personality. They questioned the extent to which these qualities can be learned. Examples of qualities placed in this category include "is open-minded," "has a sense of humor," "integrity," "honesty," "high energy level," and "is diplomatic." Some qualities might require the completion of a formal degree program. The following analysis omits the categories of character and formal education.

To make the list of qualities most useful, Table 8.1 groups the remaining qualities and the choices rated by the respondents, using the same headings shown in chapter 6—the categories of external policy/citizens of university/community (for public librarians), resource development, library culture, and strategic direction.

ARL Libraries

Part A of Table 8.1 provides a relative ranking of each category as a means for "best acquiring" a quality. Work experience was most frequently mentioned. However, for the areas of knowledge, work experience and leadership institutes were the most mentioned, although respondents did note that formal education programs and continuing education programs could play a supporting role. It is interesting to note that leadership institutes scored the highest for "is committed to staff diversity (and is culturally sensitive)," "intellectual property rights," "facilitates the group process," "develops a campus visibility for the library," "outcomes (and accreditation) assessment," "information literacy," "scholarly communication," "trends in higher education," "digital libraries," "fundraising," "service quality measurement," "understands the complex environment in which the library functions," and "teaching and learning theory."

ACRL Libraries

Part B of Table 8.1 addresses academic libraries other than those belonging to the ARL. The respondents also emphasized work experience but they mentioned how their past educational programs affected their leadership

Table 8.1
Ways to Acquire the Qualities

A. Association of Research Libraries

Qualities	External/Policy/ Citizen of University/Campus Community	Resource Development	Library Culture	Strategic Direction
Is committed to service			WE (3.3) M (4) LI (2.5)	WE (3.3) M (4) LI (2.5)
Is results oriented		WE (4.0) M (3.3)	WE (4.0) M (3.3)	WE (4.0) M (3.3)
Communicates effec- tively with staff			WE (3.8) M (3.8)	
Delegates authority			WE (5.0) M (4.2) LI (2.5)	
Facilitates a productive work environment			WE (5.0) M (0.8)	
Is willing to make tough decisions			WE (4.2) M (4.2) LI (2.5)	
Promotes professional growth in staff			WE −(4.2) M (4.2)	
Manages fiscal re- sources/budgets			WE (5.0)	
Engages in fundraising and donor relations		WE (4.3) M (4.3)		
Nurtures the develop- ment of new pro- grams and services/ refines existing ones as needed			WE (4.5) M (4.5) LI (2.7)	WE (4.5) M (4.5) LI (2.7)
Develops various sources of funding		WE (4.7)		
Is committed to staff diversity (and is cul- turally sensitive)			WE (3.7) M (2.8) LI (4.5)	

Note: WE = Work Experience; M = Mentoring; and LI = Leadership Institute. The scale ranged from 1 (minimally) to 5 (entirely).

Table 8.1
Ways to Acquire the Qualities (continued)

A. Association of Research Libraries (continued)

Qualities	External/Policy/ Citizen of University/Campus Community	Resource Development	Library Culture	Strategic Direction
Ensures that planned action is implemented and evaluated			WE (4.7) M (0.5)	
Facilitates the group process			WE (4.7) M (3.8) LI (3.3)	
Resolves conflicts			WE (3.5) M (3.5) LI (0.8)	
Builds a shared vision for the library	WE (4.7) M (0.5) LI −(0.8)			
Manages/shapes change			WE (4.7) M (3.0) LI (3.2)	
Is able to function in a political environment	WE (3.0) M (3.0) LI (3.0)			
Develops a campus visibility for the library	WE (3.8) M (3.8) LI (3.8)			
Is an advocate for librarians' role in higher education	M (0.5) LI (3.0)			
Thinks "outside the box" (in new and creative ways applicable to the problem)			WE (0.5) M (3.0) LI (0.5)	
Builds consensus in carrying out strategic directions			WE (4.7) M (0.5)	WE (4.7) M (0.5)
Leads and participates in consortia and cooperative endeavors				WE (3.0) M (0.5)

Note: WE = Work Experience; M = Mentoring; and LI = Leadership Institute. The scale ranged from 1 (minimally) to 5 (entirely).

Table 8.1
Ways to Acquire the Qualities (continued)

A. Association of Research Libraries (continued)

Qualities	External/Policy/ Citizen of University/Campus Community	Resource Development	Library Culture	Strategic Direction
Is collaborative	WE (2.5)		WE (2.5)	
Is entrepreneurial		WE (2.5) M (2.5)		
Brings issues of broad importance to the university community, fostering wide discussion and action, when appropriate	WE (3.8) M (3.8) LI (3.8)			
Demonstrates effective networking skills				WE (3.8) M (3.8) LI (0.5)
Keeps the library focused on its mission			WE (3.3)	
Changes/shapes the library's culture			WE (3.3)	
Develops and fosters partnerships with groups and organizations on/off campus	WE (2.5) M (0.8)			
Leads in a shared decision-making environment	WE (3.5) M (3.5) LI (2.5)			
Sets priorities			WE (4.2)	
Plans for life cycles of information technologies and services			WE (3.3)	
Responds to needs of various constituencies				WE (3.3) M (3.3)

Note: WE = Work Experience; M = Mentoring; and LI = Leadership Institute. The scale ranged from 1 (minimally) to 5 (entirely).

Table 8.1
Ways to Acquire the Qualities (continued)

A. Association of Research Libraries (continued)

Qualities	External/Policy/ Citizen of University/Campus Community	Resource Development	Library Culture	Strategic Direction
Creates and implements systems that assess the library's value to its users				LI (3.3)
Creates an environment that fosters accountability			WE (4.2) M (0.8) LI (1.7)	
Has credibility			WE (3.8) M (0.8)	
Is accessible			WE (4.0) M (0.5)	
Is able to work effectively in groups			WE (3.7) M (3.7) LI (2.5)	
Has self-awareness of strengths and weaknesses			WE (1.3) M (2.5)	
Analyzes and solves problems			WE (3.3) M (3.3) LI (2.5)	
Has a variety of work experiences			WE (3.3) M (0.8)	
Has a broad knowledge of issues	WE (3.8) M (0.3) LI (3.3)		WE (3.8) M (0.3) LI (3.3)	
Manages time effectively	WE (3.5) M (2.8) LI (2.5)		WE (3.5) M (2.8) LI (2.5)	
Articulates direction for the library			WE (3.2) M (0.2) LI (2.5)	WE (3.2) M (0.2) LI (2.5)
Has organizational agility			WE (4.2)	

Note: WE = Work Experience; M = Mentoring; and LI = Leadership Institute. The scale ranged from 1 (minimally) to 5 (entirely).

Table 8.1
Ways to Acquire the Qualities (continued)

A. Association of Research Libraries (continued)

Qualities	External/Policy/ Citizen of University/Campus Community	Resource Development	Library Culture	Strategic Direction
Understands that one does not have all the answers			WE (4.2) M (3.3) LI (3.3)	
Is an enabler and facilitator			WE (3.3) M (2.5) LI (2.5)	
Has team-building skills			WE (3.3) M (2.5) LI (2.5)	
Scholarly communication	LI (3.3)	LI (3.3)	LI (3.3)	LI (3.3)
Understands the complex environment in which the library functions			WE (4.2) M (3.3) LI (3.3)	
Knowledge of financial management			WE (4.2) LI (0.8)	
Facilities planning (including remote storage and multi-use buildings)			WE (4.2) LI (3.3)	
Digital libraries		WE (2.8) LI (3.3)	WE (2.8) LI (3.3)	
Planning (strategic, long-term)				WE (2.5) M (2.5) LI (2.5)
Trends in higher education	LI (3.3)			
Information technology	WE (4.2) LI (4.2)	WE (4.2) LI (4.2)	WE (4.2) LI (4.2)	WE (4.2) LI (4.2)
Management issues			WE (4.2) M (5.0) LI (4.2)	
Outcomes (and accreditation) assessment	M (0.8) LI (3.5)		M (0.8) LI (3.5)	M (0.8) LI (3.5)

Note: WE = Work Experience; M = Mentoring; and LI = Leadership Institute. The scale ranged from 1 (minimally) to 5 (entirely).

Table 8.1
Ways to Acquire the Qualities (continued)

A. Association of Research Libraries (continued)

Qualities	External/Policy/ Citizen of University/Campus Community	Resource Development	Library Culture	Strategic Direction
User expectations/information needs	WE (3.3) LI (3.3)		WE (3.3) LI (3.3)	WE (3.3) LI (3.3)
Intellectual property rights	M (0.8) LI (4.2)		M (0.8) LI (4.2)	M (0.8) LI (4.2)
Fundraising		WE (4.3) M (1.5) LI (3.3)		
Community's view of the library	WE (4.5) M (0.3)			WE (4.5) M (0.3)
Public relations	WE (3.0) M (0.5) LI (2.5)			WE (3.0) M (0.5) LI (2.5)
Service quality measurement			WE (3.2) M (0.7) LI (3.3)	WE (3.2) M (0.7) LI (3.3)
Goals (educational, research, and service) of the parent institution	WE (5.0) M (0.8) LI (0.8)			
Information delivery systems			WE (4.3) M (0.8) LI (0.8)	
Publishing industry		WE (3.3) LI (4.2)	WE (3.3) LI (4.2)	
Resource sharing				WE (4.2) M (0.8) LI (4.2)
Information literacy			WE (0.5) LI (4.2)	WE (0.5) LI (4.2)
Teaching and learning theory			WE (0.5) LI (3.3)	

Note: WE = Work Experience; M = Mentoring; and LI = Leadership Institute. The scale ranged from 1 (minimally) to 5 (entirely).

Table 8.1
Ways to Acquire the Qualities (continued)

B. Other Academic Libraries

Qualities	External/Policy/ Citizen of University/Campus Community	Resource Development	Library Culture	Strategic Direction
Has supervisory experience			WE (4.2) M (1.4) LI (1.6)	
Has proven managerial ability in personnel, fiscal, budgetary, and program assessment matters		WE (4.0) M −(2.3) LI (1.7)	WE (4.0) M (2.3) LI (1.7)	
Is able to plan, implement, and evaluate strategic goals				WE (4.0) M (2.1) LI (2.1)
Is able to work in collegial, networked environment			WE (4.0) M (3.0) LI (1.9)	
Understands and is committed to institutional mission				WE (4.0) M (1.9) LI (1.6)
Has proven facilitative leadership skills	WE (3.7) M (2.4) LI (2.6)		WE (3.7) M (2.4) LI (2.6)	
Has proven ability to foster team building and participatory management			WE (3.6) M (2.4) LI (2.6)	
Has a record of innovative and effective leadership	WE (3.6) M (2.6) LI (1.7)		WE (3.6) M (2.6) LI (1.7)	
Has firm commitment to quality	WE (4) M (2.3) LI (1.9)		WE (4) M (2.3) LI (1.9)	
Has a vision in formulating programs and implementing strategies to integrate print and electronic resources				WE −(3.7) M −(2.7) LI (2.9)

Note: WE = Work Experience; M = Mentoring; and LI = Leadership Institute. The scale ranged from 1 (minimally) to 5 (entirely).

Table 8.1
Ways to Acquire the Qualities (continued)

B. Other Academic Libraries (continued)

Qualities	External/Policy/ Citizen of University/Campus Community	Resource Development	Library Culture	Strategic Direction
Has experience in positions of increasing responsibility			WE (4.9) M (1.1) LI (1.0)	
Has demonstrated ability to identify trends				WE (3.7) M −(2.1) LI (2.6)
Has experience in developing digital libraries			WE (4.0) M (1.1) LI (0.9)	WE (4.0) M (1.1) LI (0.9)
Is able to serve as an advocate for library (develops, articulates, and communicates a rationale for the library)	WE (4.6) M (2.6) LI (1.4)			
Has excellent oral and written communication skills	WE (4.6) M (2.1) LI (1.0)		WE (4.6) M (2.1) LI (1.0)	
Is able to work collaboratively with campus colleagues	WE (4.0) M (2.3) LI (1.0)			
Is able to articulate vision for library within the institution				WE (3.4) M (1.7) LI (1.1)
Has demonstrated ability to exercise mature judgment			WE (2.6) M (2.1) LI (0.9)	
Is committed to professional development of library personnel			WE (2.7) M (1.9) LI (2.0)	
Has a documented record of problem solving			WE (2.9) M (1.9) LI (1.3)	
Has knowledge of library operations			WE (4.7) M (1.0) LI (0.4)	

Note: WE = Work Experience; M = Mentoring; and LI = Leadership Institute. The scale ranged from 1 (minimally) to 5 (entirely).

Table 8.1
Ways to Acquire the Qualities (continued)

B. Other Academic Libraries (continued)

Qualities	External/Policy/ Citizen of University/Campus Community	Resource Development	Library Culture	Strategic Direction
Has experience with change management			WE (3.3) M (3.0) LI (2.3)	
Has experience with current technology and information systems as they apply to libraries	WE (4.7) M (1.0) LI (1.1)	WE (4.7) M (1.0) LI (1.1)	WE (4.7) M (1.0) LI (1.1)	WE (4.7) M (1.0) LI (1.1)
Has experience with program assessment and evaluation	WE (4.3) M (1.4) LI (2.4)		WE (4.3) M (1.4) LI (2.4)	
Has experience with information technology	WE (4.4) M (1.0) LI (1.0)	WE (4.4) M (1.0) LI (1.0)	WE (4.4) M (1.0) LI (1.0)	WE (4.4) M (1.0) LI (1.0)
Has experience with planning: strategic, technology, collection development, marketing, facilities, security, personnel development, and fundraising			WE (4.0) M (2.0) LI (3.4)	WE (4.0) M (2.0) LI (3.4)
Has experience with collaborative arrangements between/among multi-campus and statewide settings and other institutions	WE (4.1) M (2.1) LI (2.0)		WE (4.1) M (2.1) LI (2.0)	WE (4.1) M (2.1) LI (2.0)
Has experience with scholarly communication	WE (4.1) M (2.6) LI (3.7)	WE (4.1) M (2.6) LI (3.7)	WE (4.1) M (2.6) LI (3.7)	WE (4.1) M (2.6) LI − (3.7)
Has experience with public relations	WE (4.3) M (2.0) LI (3.1)			WE (4.3) M (2.0) LI (3.1)

Note: WE = Work Experience; M = Mentoring; and LI = Leadership Institute. The scale ranged from 1 (minimally) to 5 (entirely).

Table 8.1
Ways to Acquire the Qualities (continued)

B. Other Academic Libraries (continued)

Qualities	External/Policy/ Citizen of University/Campus Community	Resource Development	Library Culture	Strategic Direction
Has knowledge of collection development			WE (4.4) M (2.0) LI (0.9)	
Has experience with marketing of services and resources	WE (4.0) M (2.3) LI (3.4)		WE (4.0) M (2.3) LI (3.4)	WE (4.0) M (2.3) LI (3.4)
Has record of scholarly achievement	WE (4.6) M (2.6) LI (0.9)		WE (4.6) M (2.6) LI (0.9)	
Has proven fundraising capabilities and success in securing funding support		WE (4.3) M (2.3) LI (3.1)		
Has experience with information literacy	WE (4.0) M (1.6) LI (1.9)		WE (4.0) M (1.6) LI (1.9)	WE (4.0) M (1.6) LI (1.9)
Has knowledge of bibliographic control			WE (4.4) M (1.4) LI (3.1)	
Has experience in managing or planning digital libraries	WE (4.4) M (0.9) LI (3.1)	WE (4.4) M (0.9) LI (3.1)	WE (4.4) M (0.9) LI (3.1)	WE (4.4) M (0.9) LI (3.1)
Has experience with grant writing		WE (4.3) M (2.3) LI (0.9)		WE (4.3) M (2.3) LI (0.9)
Has experience in planning or coordinating new library building projects			WE (4.4) M (2.7) LI (1.9)	WE (4.4) M (2.7) LI (1.9)
Has expertise with distance education	WE (4.6) M (2.7) LI (2.7)	WE (4.6) M (2.7) LI (2.7)	WE (4.6) M (2.7) LI (2.7)	WE (4.6) M (2.7) LI (2.7)

Note: WE = Work Experience; M = Mentoring; and LI = Leadership Institute. The scale ranged from 1 (minimally) to 5 (entirely).

Table 8.1
Ways to Acquire the Qualities (continued)

C. Public Libraries

Qualities	External/Policy/ Citizen of University/Campus Community	Resource Development	Library Culture	Strategic Direction
Is able to work effectively with library boards	WE (3.6) M (1.4) LI (1.2)			
Is able to communicate effectively with staff			WE (3.6) M (1.0) LI (1.4)	
Is able to work effectively with staff			WE (3.6) M (1.4) LI (1.4)	
Is an advocate for the library with (1) community/civic and (2) government agencies/organizations	WE (4.2) M (1.6) LI (1.8)			
Is able to articulate/ communicate the vital role of the library to the community and to government	WE (4.2) M (1.4) LI (1.6)			
Is able to engage in effective problem solving			WE (3.4) M (1.4) LI (2.0)	
Is able to work effectively with community/civic organizations	WE (3.4) M −(1.2) LI (2.2)			
Is able to work effectively with friends' groups	WE (3.6) M (1.2) LI (2.0)			
Is able to work effectively with state and local public officials	WE (3.4) M (1.2) LI −(1.2)			

Note: WE = Work Experience; M = Mentoring; and LI = Leadership Institute. The scale ranged from 1 (minimally) to 5 (entirely).

Table 8.1
Ways to Acquire the Qualities (continued)

C. Public Libraries (continued)

Qualities	External/Policy/ Citizen of University/Campus Community	Resource Development	Library Culture	Strategic Direction
Is willing to involve staff in planning and development of services			WE (3.4) M (1) LI (1.2)	
Is able to develop long-range plans in collaboration with library's community	WE (3.6) M (1.6) LI (2.0)			WE (3.6) M (1.6) LI (2.0)
Has good team-building skills			WE (3.4) M (1.2) LI (2.2)	
Is willing to further the professional development of staff			WE (3.4) M (1.2) LI (1.8)	
Is willing to encourage board and other community members to be advocates	WE (4.2) M (1.2) LI (2.0)			
Is able to work effectively with a union	WE (3.2) M (1.2) LI (1.2)		WE (3.2) M (1.2) LI (1.2)	WE (3.2) M (1.2) LI (1.2)
Advocates for the library with individual constituents	WE (3.4) M (1.2) LI (2.0)			
Is able to work effectively with the general public	WE (3.6) M (1.0) LI (1.4)			
Has good time-management skills			WE (3.6) M (1) LI (1.4)	
Has good understanding of job assignments and workflow			WE (4.8) M (1) LI (1.8)	
Appreciates importance of marketing/public relations	WE (3.2) M (1.2) LI (1.8)			WE (3.2) M (1.2) LI (1.8)

Note: WE = Work Experience; M = Mentoring; and LI = Leadership Institute. The scale ranged from 1 (minimally) to 5 (entirely).

Table 8.1
Ways to Acquire the Qualities (continued)

C. Public Libraries (continued)

Qualities	External/Policy/ Citizen of University/Campus Community	Resource Development	Library Culture	Strategic Direction
Is able to manage all facets of library operations			WE (4.8) M (0.6) LI (0.2)	
Has progressive admin- istrative/manage- rial/supervisory ex- perience			WE (4.2) M (0) LI (0.4)	
Is able to integrate technology into the library			WE (3.8) M (0.4) LI (1.2)	
Has an appropriate number of years of professional experi- ence (reflecting pro- gressive managerial responsibilities)			WE (5.0)	
Is able to design out- reach services			WE (2.8) M (0.6) LI (1.6)	WE (2.8) M (0.6) LI (1.6)
Has a vision of the vital role that the library plays in the commu- nity	WE (3) M (0.6) LI (1)			
Demonstrates effective oral and written communication skills	WE (3.0) M (0.6) LI (1)		WE (3.0) M (0.6) LI (1)	
Demonstrates excellent interpersonal/people skills	WE (2.8) M (0.6) LI (1.2)		WE (2.8) M (0.6) LI (1.2)	
Exhibits a strong com- mitment to public service			WE (3.0) M (0) LI (1.2)	WE (3.0) M (0) LI (1.2)
Is comfortable with di- verse populations	WE (4.0) M (0.2) LI (1)		WE (4.0) M (0.2) LI (1)	

Note: WE = Work Experience; M = Mentoring; and LI = Leadership Institute. The scale ranged from 1 (minimally) to 5 (entirely).

162

Table 8.1
Ways to Acquire the Qualities (continued)

C. Public Libraries (continued)

Qualities	External/Policy/ Citizen of University/Campus Community	Resource Development	Library Culture	Strategic Direction
Has good organizational skills			WE (3) M (0.8) LI (1)	
Projects a professional manner	WE (2.6) M (0.6) LI (0.6)		WE (2.6) M (0.6) LI (0.6)	
Is able to demonstrate innovative leadership	WE (2.2) M (1) LI −(1.2)		WE (2.2) M (1) LI (1.2)	
Furthers own professional development			WE (3.2) M (0.4) LI (1)	
Trends and innovations in libraries			WE (3) M (0.8) LI (1.8)	
Current library practices			WE (3.2) M (0.8) LI (1.8)	
Long-term planning			WE (3.4) M (0.6) LI (1.8)	
Budgeting and financial planning		WE (3.0) M (0.6) LI (1.8)		
Intellectual freedom	WE (2.8) M (0.8) LI (1.4)		WE (2.8) M (0.8) LI (1.4)	WE (2.8) M (0.8) LI (1.4)
Law and public policy issues relevant to public libraries	WE (4.2) M (0.4) LI (1.6)			WE (4.2) M (0.4) LI (1.6)
Demographic changes in the community				WE (3.6) M (0.4) LI −(2.2)
Economic changes in the community				WE (3.4) M (0.4) LI (2.2)

Note: WE = Work Experience; M = Mentoring; and LI = Leadership Institute. The scale ranged from 1 (minimally) to 5 (entirely).

Table 8.1
Ways to Acquire the Qualities (continued)

C. Public Libraries (continued)

Qualities	External/Policy/ Citizen of University/Campus Community	Resource Development	Library Culture	Strategic Direction
Functions of library boards	WE (2.8) M (0.4) LI (2.2)			
Roles of state/local public officials	WE (2.6) M (0.8) LI (1.8)			
Functions of friends' groups	WE (3.4) M (1) LI (2.6)			
Knowledge of the general public	WE (4) M (1) LI (1.8)			
Community analysis				WE (3.4) M (1.2) LI (2.4)
Emerging technological trends				WE (2.6) M (1.2) LI (3.0)
Building and remodeling			WE (3.2) M (1) LI (2.6)	
Concepts of collection development			WE (3) M (1.2) LI (3.2)	
Project management			WE (2.6) M (1.2) LI (2)	
Current human resources administration/personnel administration			WE (3.0) M (1) LI (2.2)	
Measurement and evaluation methods			WE (2.6) M (1.4) LI (2.8)	
Library public services			WE (3.0) M (1.4) LI (2.8)	

Note: WE = Work Experience; M = Mentoring; and LI = Leadership Institute. The scale ranged from 1 (minimally) to 5 (entirely).

Table 8.1
Ways to Acquire the Qualities (continued)

C. Public Libraries (continued)

Qualities	External/Policy/ Citizen of University/Campus Community	Resource Development	Library Culture	Strategic Direction
Library technical services			WE (3.0) M (1.4) LI (2.8)	
Trends and innovations in education				WE (2.4) M (1) LI (3.2)
Major foreign language(s) of community	WE (3.0) M (1.0) LI (2.6)			WE (3.0) M (1.0) LI (2.6)

Note: WE = Work Experience; M = Mentoring; and LI = Leadership Institute. The scale ranged from 1 (minimally) to 5 (entirely).

development. For instance, coursework culminating in the master's of business administration deals with one's "ability to plan, implement, and assess strategic goals." Two respondents explained how membership and involvement in the Digital Library Federation contributed to their knowledge of digital libraries. One explained that volunteer experiences improved one's "ability with personnel, fiscal, budgetary, and program matters."

Public Libraries

Part C of Table 8.1 covers public library directors. Although none of the options is highly rated, work experience was most mentioned. On the whole, neither mentoring nor leadership institutes had much impact. It may be that there are more opportunities for self-development in academic libraries.

Common Themes

In effect, the eighteen respondents divided the choices for meeting a set of qualities into the following seven choices:

1. An individual's character, belief and value system, upbringing, socialization, and personality;
2. Work experience;
3. Mentoring;

4. Leadership institutes;

5. Membership in professional associations (e.g., the Digital Library Federation);

6. Workshops and continuing education programs (in part, refers back to choice five); and

7. Completion of formal degree programs (MLS and other).

The first choice might be influenced by a good course or workshop on ethics and values. Qualities such as "good listening skills" can now be refined through exercises, workshops, and continuing education programs. Life experiences may also influence one's vision of the organization. For public library directors, foreign language proficiency might be gained through formal coursework, continuing education and other programs, and contact with different cultures (e.g., through extensive travel). The non–ARL library directors were the most likely to mention their attendance in workshops and continuing education programs.

Complicating any clear-cut division among the choices, one respondent noted that an individual's personality, for instance, might play a small role in one's ability to work effectively with external groups and with staff, in being able to motivate staff, and in projecting a professional manner. Furthermore, personal initiative somewhat influences the quality of having progressive administrative/managerial/supervisory experience, and one's belief or value system impacts one's willingness to engage in community service. Education, either continuing education or a formal degree program, most likely relates to the acquisition of the areas of knowledge, those related to management. One respondent, who holds a Ph.D. degree, believed that the coursework for that degree was "quite helpful" for dealing with scholarly communication.

Given these caveats, one respondent fairly well summarized the sentiment of the others: "Generally, I think work experience contributes most to gaining the qualities. While mentoring and workshop/institutes can help highlight needed skills, I think they largely help if the ability or skill is already there. Also, whatever experience, mentoring, etc., is available, a lot of one's ability goes back to his or her personality, temperament, and values."

Seeing that respondents infrequently mentioned formal degree programs, we subsequently asked a couple of them about such programs. They saw Ph.D. programs as focusing on research and not leadership or the type of program addressed in Figure 8.1. Master's programs in business administration focus on knowledge of management but not its application to libraries and not all the aspects of leadership identified in chapter 6. One respondent noted that the business courses he took provided a foundation with leadership, but he still felt that "leadership has more to do with personality characteristics than any information or formal training/education program. The formal programs and experience tend to enhance and sharpen what is already there." Another respondent mentioned that library school curricula and ALA conferences introduce people to a number of issues and knowledge areas.

"The library school provides a basic introduction that might be supplemented by conference programs." The rest of the respondents thought that directors needed more than a "basic introduction."

Naturally, a director's knowledge and how it was acquired depends on the job assignments successfully handled prior to assuming a directorship. Clearly, further research should explore those assignments and the career paths that individuals took to reach a directorship and as they advanced from one directorship to another.

Another respondent stressed the importance of

ego and personality traits for those items that dealt with people issues and for skills that are developed prior to becoming a director. For example, no one with an *unhealthy* ego—a very controlling person—is likely to exhibit any sincere teambuilding skills or be willing to further the professional development of staff in general as opposed to his or her sycophants. The prior skills would include organizational skills and time management. These have to be developed as one matures.

Finally, in comparing the ratings for parts A through C (Table 8.1), it is apparent that those responding to the public library survey had the most disagreement in their ratings. They also were the harshest as they provided the lowest ratings. Clearly, this finding merits further investigation and review.

For further reflection on the table, we asked three directors to comment on the ratings. They were not surprised that ARL directors scored the options much higher. They felt that these directors have more developed lines of communication and interaction with their peers; their peers comprise less than 130 academic institutions. They "operate at a higher level of sophistication and deal with issues that affect ARL libraries. They also have opportunities to work with each other on a smaller set of issues and are invited to continue their dialogue in other venues such as the OCLC research group. Other library directors are more likely to deal with directors in more diverse, dissimilar settings. This is especially true in professional organizations." They were not surprised that work experience was rated much higher than the other options. As one director explained, "people are too busy to engage in mentoring. They cannot commit the necessary time to do it properly. Too often, we see mentoring done on the 'fly.'"

When asked for their opinion about the grouping of respondents into categories of ARL directors, ACRL directors, and public library directors, they explained that they understood why we made that selection for an exploratory study. However, they recommended that any further comparison of academic institutions be based on the Carnegie Classification of Institutions of Higher Education, developed by the Carnegie Foundation for the Advancement of Teaching.[14] In this way, responses could be compared within groups of similar institutions (e.g., those with a similar number of students served and graduate programs offered) and, as a result, the ratings might be, as one respondent said, more "insightful."

STATE-LEVEL LEADERSHIP INITIATIVES

Following the examples of the national leadership training programs, there have been many similar programs developed at the regional and state levels. Regional programs include those sponsored by the Mountain Plains Library Association and the Southeastern Institute for Collaborative Leadership, a multisponsor project supported by the Council on Library and Information Resources, the Institute of Museum and Library Services, SOLINET, and each of the ten southeastern state libraries. More than a dozen individual states have launched leadership training initiatives: California, Colorado, Illinois, Iowa, Maryland, Massachusetts, Michigan, Missouri, Nebraska, Nevada, New Jersey, Ohio, Texas, Utah, and Wyoming. Training institutes are generally two- to five-day experiences that are conducted by prominent leadership consultants, both from within the library profession and from other areas.

Multiple outcomes have been identified for these learning institutes. In Massachusetts, the leadership program, YSLead, identifies sixty potential leaders in school and public libraries, together with twelve mentors for two and one-half days of collaborative training in leadership and mentoring. Topics addressed by the consultant include understanding of leadership styles, the role of the leader, communication, coaching, and mentoring. The Tall Texans Leadership Development Institute, almost a decade old, provides leadership training for the Texas Library Association membership by offering an annual leadership development institute for librarians and laypersons. The institute is designed to foster leadership capabilities, define leadership development activities for Texas Library Association members, and expand cultural diversity in library leadership. The Tall Texans program is particularly designed for midcareer library and information science practitioners (with or without degrees) who are ready for new leadership responsibilities. In a typical institute, twenty-four participants and six mentors join to engage in activities such as change-agent behavior, communication styles, conflict management, styles of leadership, mentoring and management, self-awareness of strengths, personnel planning, developing a shared vision of the organization, understanding group dynamics, team building, and workplace values.

The Illinois State Library, in partnership with the Illinois Library Association, launched an ambitious leadership initiative, Synergy, in 2002.[15] The Synergy program may be nationally unique in that the participants and mentors meet for three two-and-one-half-day sessions per year. A maximum of thirty MLS librarians will participate in the yearlong program, which will "focus on self-assessment; discovering and developing personal values; identifying the local, state, and global environment; fostering and expanding skills and tools for personal, professional, and positional leadership; creating a cohort group; establishing mentor relationships; and developing a vision of the future of Illinois librarianship." Synergy is broadly supported within the state's leadership community, and has garnered high marks for its inaugural experience. Additional states will surely follow along this path and develop programs of their own. The regional approach should also receive support, because it draws participants from a variety of states and thereby introduces new perspectives. One outcome over the years may be employment in more than one type of library during a career, a choice not frequently made at present. Another approach, over time, would be for various leadership institutes to specialize in such areas as values clarification, conflict resolution, and strategic planning.

CONCLUSION

There are definitely many ways for individuals to gain knowledge about, and mastery of, the qualities identified in previous chapters. From the ratings in Table 8.1, it is apparent that ARL directors, through the Association of Research Libraries and other venues, have the most opportunities to update their knowledge and skill sets. It may also be that contact with AULs in their own organizations exerts some influence. However, this speculation is worthy of additional investigation as this chapter only reports initial (exploratory) research that others could pursue. Furthermore, the success of any approach may rely on the human factor. In other words, part of the success of leadership institutes may be the instructors and one's peers in the cohort. Those individuals in a cohort might bond, develop friendships, and share knowledge. The same is true of the mentor/mentee relationship; it depends on finding a good match and on how busy both parties are with other activities. Finally, work experience requires opportunities to pursue different assignments and problems, and to gain more diverse knowledge, as well as finding individuals willing and able to share their own knowledge and experiences. At the same time, the mentor needs to challenge the mentee to continue to develop and explore. In effect, acquiring a set of qualities depends on finding the right learning experiences. Those experiences may not be the same for everyone. However, chapter 7 offers some guidance about how to get started.

> The quality of leadership in an organization seldom exceeds that of the person at the top.[16]

NOTES

1. William Knott, "Public Library Leadership: Meetings and Mechanics of Growth," *Colorado Libraries* 23 (summer 1997): 30.
2. See the home page of the Association of Research Libraries, Office of Leadership and Management Services (available: http://www.arl/org/olms/index.html; http://www.arl.org/training/index.html).
3. See Mark D. Winston and Teresa Y. Neely, "Leadership Development and Public Libraries," *Public Library Quarterly* 19, no. 3 (2001): 15–32.
4. This Canadian institute covers leadership and introduces participants to "risk-taking, creativity, communication, change, power, and styles of leadership." It

also addresses topics such as group work, team building, and collegiality, and invites professional leaders to act as mentors at the five-day institute; see the Northern Exposure to Leadership Web site (available: http://www.ls.ualberta.ca/neli/instit.html).

5. Frye Institute, *Leading the Information Revolution in Twenty-First-Century Higher Education* (Atlanta, Ga.: Frye Institute, 2002) (promotional pamphlet).

6. Urban Libraries Council, "Executive Leadership Institute" (Evanston, Ill.: Urban Libraries Council, 2002) (available: http://www.urbanlibraries.org/). The Urban Libraries Council also conducts surveys of the skills that directors of urban libraries need.

7. Gordon F. Shea, *Mentoring: Helping Employees Reach Their Full Potential* (New York: American Management Association, AMA Membership Publications Division, 1994), 13. See also Association of Research Libraries, *Mentoring Programs in ARL Libraries,* SPEC Kit 239 (Washington, D.C.: Association of Research Libraries, March 1999) (available: http://www.arl.org/spec/239fly.html).

8. Association of Research Libraries, *Mentoring Programs in ARL Libraries,* 3.

9. Ibid.

10. See Larry Hardesty, "College Library Directors Mentor Program: 'Passing It On': A Personal Reflection," *The Journal of Academic Librarianship* 23 (July 1997): 281–90. See also Austin College, "The College Library Directors Mentor Program" (available: http://www.austinc.edu/CLS/colment.html).

11. Austin College, "The College Library Directors Mentor Program," 1–2.

12. See the NLM/AAHSL Leadership Fellows Program, which is a program offered in cooperation with ARL's Office of Leadership and Management Services (October 2002) (available: see http://www.arl/olms/fellows/).

13. See Peter Hernon and Robert E. Dugan, *An Action Plan for Outcomes Assessment in Your Library* (Chicago: American Library Association, 2002), 101–18.

14. See the Carnegie Foundation for the Advancement of Teaching, *The Carnegie Classification of Institutions of Higher Education* (Menlo Park, Calif.: Carnegie Foundation for the Advancement of Teaching, 2001).

15. Patricia Norris, "Bringing Synergy to Leadership," *Interface* 24 [published by Association of Specialized and Cooperative Library Agencies] (spring 2002): 2. The same issue has other short articles on various state library leadership initiatives.

16. John H. Zenger and Joseph Folkman, *The Extraordinary Leader: Turning Good Managers into Great Leaders* (New York: McGraw-Hill, 2002), 27.

9

⋯

HUNTING HEADS
AND FINAL REFLECTIONS

Vision management demands intuition and courage.[1]

For years, the library community has investigated the knowledge, skills, competencies, and attitudes expected of library and information studies professionals. Although much of the research and discussion has focused on those individuals entering the profession, there has also been extensive discussion of the qualities essential for library directors. As shown in chapter 2, there is a significant literature on the topic, especially as some authors have speculated about whether a crisis looms in filling future positions with individuals adequately prepared for leadership positions. Traditionally, preparation has been gained from on-the-job experience and mentoring. Individuals seeking directorships may have participated in leadership institutes, but these programs tend to be episodic; they provide short-term coverage of selected issues. As indicated in chapter 8, more sustained educational roles will have to come from specialized programs outside of the profession (e.g., master's programs in business administration) or doctoral programs; however, doctoral programs focus on contributing to basic and applied research, not the mastery of qualities directly related to the managerial and leadership qualities expected of library directors, as shown in Figure 8.1. Therefore, new opportunities must become available, and their direct relevance in providing the expected qualities must be demonstrated.

Billy E. Frye, chancellor of Emory University, in a paper presented in Ann Arbor, Michigan on October 29, 1999, remarked that when Otto von Bismarck took command of the Prussian army in 1871, he began searching for leaders.[2] In order to identify potential leaders, he reviewed the personnel files of all of his officers and divided them into four categories: (1) those who were capable and ambitious; (2) those who were capable but not ambitious; (3) those who were neither ambitious nor capable; and (4) those who were ambitious but not capable. He promoted the officers in the first group to positions of high responsibility as soon as possible; assigned the officers in the second group to middle management, where responsibility, but not initiative, was needed; put the third group in charge of remote outposts that were not important; and had the men in the fourth group shot.

Those individuals searching for the next generation of library leaders are not likely to take measures as drastic as those of von Bismarck, but there is a growing concern about the pool of future leaders. "At the March, 1988, OCLC Conference on the Future of the Public Library, participants were asked to list their worst fears and greatest hopes for the future. The most frequently mentioned fear was inadequate leadership."[3] The media and the professional literature continue to note the ever-increasing shortage of certain types of librarians, including directors, and to recognize that the large number of upcoming retirements will only exacerbate the situation. In 2001, Mark Winston stated, "One of the major issues facing [information] organizations in the 21st Century will relate to the need for effectiveness and proactive leadership."[4] A key player in future searches for outstanding library leadership will be the headhunter, already a mainstay in corporate America.

THE HEADHUNTER VORTEX

Increasingly, larger institutions of higher education and public libraries use headhunters to guide the identification of a pool of candidates from which the final selection of the university librarian or public library director will be made. A question, then, not addressed from the research reported in the previous chapters is, "Which qualities do these firms consider essential and which ones do they encourage search committees to pursue in the hiring of a new director?" And, further, what are the structural characteristics of the headhunter enterprise which library employers and emerging leaders should understand? Two recent books provide informative reading on the complex, triadic relationship among headhunters, employers, and prospective job seekers, and how each party shapes the search process—*Headhunters: Matchmaking in the Labor Market*, by William Finlay and James E. Coverdill, and *The Headhunter's Edge*, by Jeffrey E. Christian.[5]

According to Finlay and Coverdill, "headhunters are third-party agents who are paid a fee by employers for finding job candidates for them."[6] Research for this book derives from data collected during the 1990s from contingency headhunters and their clients in the southeastern United States. The team conducted thirty-four semistructured interviews with headhunters and conducted an additional 300 hours of field work involving 150 hours at 5 different headhunting firms, and additional field work consisting of attending seminars, lectures, luncheons, training sessions, and conferences sponsored by various contingency headhunter associations. Finally, more than 116 surveys were received from various headhunter firms. Headhunter clients are organizations, not candidates for jobs. In most cases, a headhunter earns a fee only if his or her candidate is the person who is hired. These headhunters work on a contingency basis and resemble other third-party agents or brokers such as real estate agents and show business agents, whose financial well-being rests on the successful promotion of a match between clients and job candidates. In addition to the contingency relationship, recruiters today are much more proactive in generating candidates for positions. There is a rather strong preference in seeking out those candidates who are currently not looking for employment, but rather are happy in their current job environment and producing at high levels.

Any discussion of the headhunter process must begin with a concise identification of the aforementioned triadic relationship and the consequences flowing from it. Finlay and Coverdill discuss this process:

We demonstrate how headhunters, although they are in a structurally weak position relative to both clients and candidates, manage not just to resist the demands of both kinds of customers but actually to assert some degree of control over them. Headhunters are vulnerable in relation to clients because they are paid on a contingency basis and operate in a highly competitive industry; they are vulnerable in relation to candidates because the latter, with whom they do not have a formal relationship, have to be talked into selling themselves. Headhunters are not nearly as helpless in practice as their structural position might suggest, however. They are quite adept at manipulating and maneuvering relations with clients and candidates in order to control their interactions, thus suggesting that frontline workers may enjoy greater informal power than is often recognized. Our analysis explains how this group of front-line service workers acquires and maintains control over their customers.

Headhunters resist customer demands through a multipronged strategy. One prong is for a headhunter to forge a long-term exclusive relationship with clients, so that clients will use this headhunter alone on search assignments. Another prong is to be selectively disloyal toward clients—to violate, under certain circumstances, the trust that clients have placed in headhunters. A third prong is to use deception to identify likely candidates and then to exploit their insecurities to become candidates. A fourth prong is to control the impression that clients and candidates form of each other before the job interview by supplying them carefully chosen information about each other; the purpose is to ensure that each party enters the interview with a positive impression with the other. A fifth prong is to require that the job offer and acceptance be channeled through the headhunter, to absorb or deflect the anger that each side might otherwise direct at the other, to alleviate their anxieties, and, if necessary, to intimidate candidates into declining counter offers.[7]

The outsourcing of the recruiting process to headhunters accelerated in the 1990s and will continue into the new century. Successful headhunters will navigate the shifting sands and prosper. Individuals who become part of the headhunter process will do well to recognize the multiple loyalties of headhunters and proceed with enthusiastic but realistic expectations. One conclusion reached by the authors is that chemistry between employers and candidates will be an increasingly important factor in the hiring process. This prediction of a workplace increasingly characterized by individuals with similar personalities may well retard progress toward diversity in the workplace. Now that we have provided a brief introduction to the organizational dynamics of headhunter agencies, let us return to the issue of leadership traits, and the identification of these traits as seen from the perspective of a seasoned headhunter.

Veteran headhunter Jeffrey E. Christian brings enviable breadth, masterful prose, and convincing insight to the subject of headhunters and defining leadership. Talent drives the economy, according to the author, and it is the talent quotient which has defined the great companies of the past several decades. There has always been a talent shortage, and the best chief executive officers have extended up to 50 percent of their time seeking and interviewing individuals in the relevant talent pool. Two such examples are Bill Gates and Jack Welch, both of whom, at important points in their company's history, devoted more than 50 percent or more of their time to this important activity. The challenge, then, is to seek out the best talent, and then create a corporate environment that no one would want to leave. Christian soon launches into his definition of leadership by noting what leadership is *not*. It is not just a personal desire to excel; it is not just hard work; it is not just a well-cut suit, a gift for gab, a scratch golf game, or a glittering resume. It is not about experience, either; no U.S. president gets a dry run at his position before election. Leadership, for Christian, requires a more subtle set of qualities, as evidenced in his "formula five" of exceptional leadership:

1. *Honesty and integrity*—Exceptional leaders are able to build a deep level of trust in organizations in a flash—an absolute requirement for turning around a company in trouble. Major change is always hard for an organization to take, and without an environment of trust change will only be resented. Leaders must ask their employees to take risks, to work under the burden of uncertainty, and to make sacrifices to ensure a better future for everyone in the company. To take a step into an abyss, people must believe that the leader is operating in their best interests and not only in his own.

2. *Intellectual firepower*—Business leaders are smart. Scary smart. They have phenomenal memories and are a storehouse of information and data. They can distill a complex situation down to the basic components for action; they can juggle multiple ideas and tasks simultaneously—and successfully. In new situations, they vacuum up the most crucial information and can see problems from different perspectives. They have an eerie ability to ask the one essential question you have not anticipated.

3. *Energy and passion*—...great leaders are not in it only for the money. They love what they do. They also know that at their level, what they do affects the lives and fortunes of thousands of employees, not to mention millions of customers and fellow citizens. The success of major companies affects the economic future of us

all. Exceptional leaders get up in the morning and head to the office with a bounce in their step, knowing that what they do can make a difference.

4. *Leadership*—A Phi Beta Kappa key will make your mother proud, but the person who is most likely to rise is the manager who's smart enough to know that he doesn't know everything and surrounds himself with talent. In my experience, what separates leaders from intelligent, enthusiastic workaholics is strong decision-making skills and the ability to take a group of diverse people with even more diverse talents and abilities and transform them into a unique corporate culture.

5. *Humility*—Exceptional leaders know what they do not know and are not afraid to admit it. In interviews I like to ask top managers this question: 'What did you do a couple of years ago that today you wished you had done better?' The best leaders have a *lot* of examples. Humble people, I have found, are people who are always learning, and good leaders must be learning all the time.[8]

Christian asserts that leadership is something that can be learned. Part of that learning process involves not being a control freak, not being autocratic, not being a bully, and not underestimating the talent that you already have. Self-assessment and emulation are valuable tools that can enhance given strengths and move to a higher plateau of leadership potential. This strong endorsement of leadership as an educable enterprise surely reaffirms the values of assessment, continuing education, and a variety of leadership learning experiences.

Outside the scope of this volume is a discussion of the skill sets which might enhance one's interaction with headhunters and potential employers. Among the many books on this subject, two of the best are *Asking the Headhunter: Reinventing the Interview to Win the Job*, by Nick A. Corcodilos; and *Knock 'Em Dead 2003*, by Martin Yate.[9]

REFLECTIONS AND A MODEST AGENDA

Our study focuses on leadership attributes as defined by library directors in three populations: midsize academic libraries, research-level academic libraries, and midsize and large public libraries. Through the progressive refinement of attributes via the Delphi process, a picture emerges of essential characteristics for the next generation of library leaders. Attributes were grouped under three headings—managerial attributes, personal attributes, and areas of knowledge. Not surprisingly, there was a close correspondence of attributes in the three main areas between and among types of libraries. Most attributes were separated by one-tenth or two-tenths of a point on a ten-point scale, making it rather difficult to isolate generalizable distinctions when such subtle gradations are present.

By way of summary, we found that, under the area of managerial attributes, ARL directors rated a commitment to service, results orientation, and communicating effectively with the staff as top qualities; ACRL directors affirmed supervisory experience, senior administrative experience, and facilitative leadership; and public library directors ranked most highly work with boards, effective work with staffs, and advocacy for the library with community/civic agencies. The choices made by the ARL directors and public library directors in this category appear to coincide more with each other than with those selected by the ACRL directors. Directors of the former two types of libraries selected attributes that have a more external orientation than did the ACRL directors. In the area of personal attributes, top personal characteristics for the ARL directors were credibility, evenhandedness, and integrity; ACRL directors emphasized problem solving, creativity, and the requirement for a master's degree in library science; and the public library directors highlighted integrity, vision of the library in the community, and oral/written communication skills. The standout difference in this comparison is that the requirement for the master's degree in library science is a very high priority for the ACRL directors.

Under the general areas of knowledge rubric, ARL library directors gave top billing to scholarly communication, understanding the complex environment in which the library functions, and knowledge of financial management. ACRL directors voted for managerial ability, experience with grant writing, and expertise in fundraising. Trends and innovations in libraries, current library practices, and long-term planning were rated most highly by the public library directors. Ranking of knowledge of the scholarly communication system is no surprise for ARL directors, but the high ratings for grant writing and fundraising may seem somewhat surprising at first glance; then again, smaller institutions may be facing proportionally more difficult fiscal times. The ratings given by public library directors clearly emphasize familiarity with current practices and innovation, perhaps linking these attributes closely to these directors' continual need to relate to internal and external constituencies.

The results for some of the lowest-rated attributes are very interesting. For ARL directors, the lowest-rated managerial qualities were resolution of conflicts and leading in a shared decision-making environment. The lowest-rated personal characteristics were good interpersonal/people skills and managing time effectively. In the general areas of knowledge, information literacy and teaching and learning theory resided in the basement of priorities. For ACRL directors, the lowest-rated managerial attributes were vision and formulating programs. Under personal attributes, high energy was rated the lowest, and under areas of knowledge, experience with scholarly communication was rated lowest. For public library directors, the lowest-scored managerial attribute was the ability to design outreach services; under personal abilities, the lowest-rated was the willingness to engage in community service; and under areas of knowledge, expertise in major foreign languages of the community received the least emphasis. The starkest contrast between ARL and ACRL library directors centers on scholarly communication, which holds a top spot on the ARL list and a bottom rung in the ACRL array. As noted in chapter 6, when the three Delphi lists were combined into a newly labeled array, some of the commonalities and divergences smoothed out, indicating a slightly different set of comparative attributes.

Some of our in-depth interviews, reported in earlier chapters, particularly the second set of ARL directors who were interviewed, provide further insight into the most desirable attributes. Rush Miller zeroes in on sharing vision, shaping change, creativity, and changing the traditional culture. Joan Giesecke places prominence on vision and optimism. For Fred Heath, one needs to enter the political environment of higher education and find worth and dignity in everyone. Miriam Drake emphasizes insight, adaptability, knowledge, trust in one's self, and intuition. Sarah Pritchard calls for courage, metaknowledge that allows seeing the big picture, and a sense of humor.

When comparing the insights from the Delphi lists and interviews with those formulated by headhunter Jeffrey Christian, there are major differences to ponder. His first choice, honesty and integrity, does coincide with top choices from the Delphi study. His number two quality, intellectual firepower, leaders as "scary smart," is not on anyone's list as an explicit characteristic. Energy and passion appear on the various lists, but not in positions of prominence. His fourth characteristic, leadership, is perhaps too diffuse to correspond to the more particular attributes identified in this study. Finally, his fifth important attribute, humility, appears in none of the lists under this wording. These differences suggest the complexity of semantic interpretation and also open the possibility that directors' self-assessment of what is needed does not closely correspond with the leadership qualities as perceived by an experienced recruiter and interviewer of senior-level executives. Additionally, the absence of generic traits on most lists (e.g., intelligence and energy) suggests further inquiry into this aspect of attribute identification.

To ensure a vital and viable professional future, librarianship must embrace a commitment to the identification, recruitment, and nurturing of the next generation of leaders. This volume represents a modest effort to ascertain core leadership qualities and to address collateral issues of self-assessment and continuing education opportunities. Much more remains to be done. Other studies should solicit the views of external university administrators, city officials, library boards, and others. Longitudinal studies of participants in leadership institutes may well illuminate the long-term value of these opportunities and suggest refinements in their content and delivery over time. Doctoral-level investigations of leadership issues in librarianship and the professions generally should be encouraged. And finally, perhaps we should not wish for a perfectly successful research outcome and a "cookie cutter" profile that would eliminate chance, diversity, and individuality.

Everyone assumes responsibility for leadership development.[10]

Leadership requires both attributes and results.[11]

NOTES

1. Pentti Sydänmaanlakka, *An Intelligent Organization: Integrating Performance, Competence and Knowledge Management* (Oxford: Capstone, 2002), 173.
2. Billy E. Frye, "Some Reflections on Universities, Libraries, and Leadership," paper presented at the University of Michigan, Ann Arbor, October 29, 1999.
3. Patrick M. O'Brien, "Quality Leadership for the Twenty-First Century." *Journal of Library Administration* 11, nos. 1 and 2 (1989): 27–34.
4. Mark D. Winston, "Recruitment Theory: Identification of Those Who Are Likely to be Successful as Leaders," *Journal of Library Administration* 32, nos. 3 and 4 (2001): 19–34.
5. William Finlay and James E. Coverdill, *Headhunters: Matchmaking in the Labor Market* (Ithaca, N.Y.: Cornell University Press, 2002); Jeffrey E. Christian, *The Headhunter's Edge* (New York: Random House, 2002). For an additional perspective and a list of attributes from a public library headhunter, see Donald J. Sager, "Evolving Virtues: Library Administrative Skills," *Public Libraries* 40 (September–October 2001): 268–72.
6. Finlay and Coverdill, *Headhunters,* 1.
7. Finlay and Coverdill, *Headhunters,* 18.
8. Christian, *The Headhunter's Edge,* 50–56.
9. Nick A. Corcodilos, *Ask the Headhunter: Reinventing the Interview to Win the Job* (New York: Dutton, 1997); Martin Yate, *Knock 'Em Dead 2003* (Avon, Mass.: Adams Media, 2002).
10. John H. Zenger and Joseph Folkman, *The Extraordinary Leader: Turning Good Managers into Great Leaders* (New York: McGraw-Hill, 2002), 220.
11. Ibid., vii.

BIBLIOGRAPHY

ARTICLES

Alire, Camila A. "Diversity and Leadership: The Color of Leadership," *Journal of Library Administration*™ 32, nos. 3 and 4 (2001): 95–109.

Alldredge, Margaret E., and Kevin J. Nilan. "3M's Leadership Competency Model: An Internally Developed Solution," *Human Resource Management* 39 (summer–fall 2000): 133–45.

Barner, Robert. "Five Steps to Leadership Competencies," *Training and Development* 54 (March 2000): 51.

Bayard, Ivy, Carol Lang, and Maureen Pastine. "Staffing Issues for Academic Libraries," *Library Issues: Briefings for Faculty and Administrators* 22 (September 2001): 1–4.

Beile, Penny M., and Megan M. Adams. "Other Duties as Assigned: Emerging Trends in the Academic Library Job Market," *College & Research Libraries* 61 (July 2000): 336–47.

Berry, John W. "Addressing the Recruitment and Diversity Crisis (President's Message)," *American Libraries* 33 (February 2002): 7.

Billups, Andrea. "Lack of Librarians," *Insight on the News* 16 (August 28, 2000): 24.

Church, Allan H., and Janine Waclawski. "The Relationship between Individual Orientation and Executive Leadership Behaviour," *Journal of Occupational and Organizational Psychology* 71 (June 1998): 99–136.

Corbus, Laurence. "Key Attributes for Library Administration," *Public Libraries* 37, no. 6 (November–December 1998): 355–56.

Dickson, Katherine Murphy. "A Work Journal," *Library Trends* 50 (Spring 2002): 687–701.

Ensman, Richard G., Jr. "Twenty-First Century Skills Quiz," *Doors and Hardware* 61 (November 1997): 60–64.

Gardner, William L., and Mark J. Martinko. "Using the Myers-Briggs Type Indicator to Study Managers: A Literature Review and Research Agenda," *Journal of Management* 22 (spring 1996): 45–84.

Goldhor, Herbert. "The Head Librarian as Administrator of a Public Library," *Illinois Libraries* 71 (September 1989): 306–13.

Goleman, Daniel. "Leadership That Gets Results," *Harvard Business Review* 78 (March 2000): 78–90.

Hardesty, Larry. "College Library Directors Mentor Program: 'Passing It On': A Personal Reflection," *The Journal of Academic Librarianship* 23 (July 1997): 281–90.

Hernon, Peter, Ronald R. Powell, and Arthur P. Young. "University Library Directors in the Association of Research Libraries: The Next Generation: Part One," *College & Research Libraries* 62 (March 2001): 116–45.

———. "University Library Directors in the Association of Research Libraries: The Next Generation: Part Two," *College & Research Libraries* 63 (January 2002): 73–90.

Hiatt, Peter. "Identifying and Encouraging Leadership Potential: Assessment Technology and the Library Profession," *Library Trends* 40 (1992): 513–42.

House, Robert J., and Ram N. Aditya. "The Social Scientific Study of Leadership: Quo Vadis?" *Journal of Management* 23 (May–June 1997): 409–74.

Kaufman, Paula T. "Where Do the Next 'We' Come From," *ARL*, no. 221 [a bimonthly report on research library issues and actions from ARL, CNI, and SPARC, published by the Association of Research Libraries, Washington, D.C.] (April 2002): 1–5.

Knott, William. "Public Library Leadership: Meetings and Mechanisms of Growth," *Colorado Libraries* 23 (summer 1997): 30–32.

Kramer, F. "CEO Briefing: On Management and Leadership," *Investor's Business Daily* (December 21, 1992): 4.

"Letters to the Editor," *The Chronicle of Higher Education* (May 10, 2002): n.p.

Lovett, Clara M. "The Dumbing Down of College Presidents," *Chronicle of Higher Education* (April 5, 2002): B2.

Lynch, Beverly P., and Kimberly Robbles Smith. "The Changing Nature of Work in Academic Libraries," *College & Research Libraries* 62 (September 2001): 407–20.

Lynch, Mary Jo. "Librarian Salaries: Annual Increase above National Average," *American Libraries* 33 (September 2002): 93.

———. "Reaching 65: Lots of Librarians Will Be There Soon," *American Libraries* 33 (March 2002): 55–56.

Mackenzie, R. Alec. "The Management Process in 3-D," *Harvard Business Review* 47 (November–December, 1969): 80–87.

Mahmoodi, Suzanne H., and Geraldine King. "Identifying Competencies and Responsibilities of Top Management Teams in Public Libraries," *Minnesota Libraries* 30 (autumn–winter 1991–92): 26–32.

Mani, Bonnie G. "Progress on the Journey to Total Quality Management: Using the Myers-Briggs Type Indicator and the Adjective Check List in Management Development," *Public Personnel Management* 24 (fall 1995): 365–401.

Martin, Susan K. "The Changing Role of the Library Director: Fund-raising and the Academic Library," *The Journal of Academic Librarianship* 24 (January 1998): 3–10.

Matarazzo, James M. "Library Human Resources: The Y2K Plus 10 Challenge," *The Journal of Academic Librarianship* 26 (July 2000): 223–24.

———. "Who Wants to Be a Millionaire (Sic Librarian!)," *The Journal of Academic Librarianship* 26 (September 2000): 309–10.

Matthews, Catherine J. "Becoming a Chief Librarian: An Analysis of Transition Stages in Academic Library Leadership," *Library Trends* 50 (spring 2002): 578–602.

McAnally, Arthur M., and Robert B. Downs. "The Changing Role of Directors of University Libraries," *College & Research Libraries* 34 (March 1973): 103–25.

McElrath, Eileen. "Challenges That Academic Library Directors Are Experiencing as Perceived by Them and Their Supervisors," *College & Research Libraries* 63 (July 2002): 304–21.

Misakian, Jo Ellen. "The 12 Pieces of Leadership," *CSLA Journal* 24 (spring 2001): 15–16.

Moran, Barbara B. "Career Patterns of Academic Library Administrators," *College & Research Libraries* 44 (September 1983): 334–44.

Morrison, Allen J. "Developing a Global Leadership Model," *Human Resource Management* 39 (summer–fall 2000): 117–31.

Norris, Patricia. "Bringing Synergy to Leadership," *Interface* 24 [published by the Association of Specialized and Cooperative Library Agencies] (spring 2002): 2.

O'Brien, Patrick M. "Quality Leadership for the Twenty-First Century," *Journal of Library Administration*™ 11, nos. 1 and 2 (1989): 27–34.

Olsgaard, John N. "Educational Preparation for Public Library Administration: A Model for Cooperation," *Journal of Library Administration*™ 11, nos. 1 and 2 (1989): 35–51.

Osborne, Reed. "Evaluation of Leadership in Ontario Public Libraries," *Canadian Journal of Information and Library Science* 21 (September–December 1996): 20–34.

Person, Ruth J., and George C. Newman. "Selection of the University Librarian," *College & Research Libraries* 51 (July 1990): 346–59.

Reser, David W., and Anita P. Schuneman. "The Academic Library Job Market: A Content Analysis Comparing Public and Technical Services," *College & Research Libraries* 53 (January 1992): 49–59.

Riggs, Donald E. "The Crisis and Opportunities in Library Leadership," *Journal of Library Administration*™ 32, nos. 3 and 4 (2001): 5–17.

———. "Editorial: Academic Library Leadership and the 'Life of the Mind,'" *College & Research Libraries* 62 (May 2001): 212–13.

Rooks, Dana C. "Terms for Academic Library Directors," *Library Trends* 43 (summer 1994): 47–61.

Rowe, Christopher. "Picking the Winners: The Thorny Issue of Assessing Leadership Potential," *Leadership and Organization Development Journal* 15 (October 1994): S1–S5.

Sager, Donald J. "Evolving Virtues: Library Administrative Skills," *Public Libraries* 40 (September–October 2001): 268–72.

Schreiber, Becky, and John Shannon. "Developing Library Leaders for the Twenty-First Century," *Journal of Library Administration™* 32, nos. 3 and 4 (2001): 35–57.

St. Lifer, Evan. "The Boomer Brain Drain: The Last of a Generation," *Library Journal* 125 (May 1, 2000): 38–42.

Stricker, Lawrence J., and Donald A. Rock. "Assessing Leadership Potential with a Biographical Measure of Personality Traits," *International Journal of Selection and Assessment* 6 (1998): 164–84.

Sweeney, Richard T. "Leadership in the Post-Hierarchical Library," *Library Trends* 43 (summer 1994): 62–94.

Totten, Herman L., and Ronald L. Keys. "The Road to Success," *Library Trends* 43 (summer 1994): 34–46.

Ulrich, D., J. Zenger, and N. Smallwood. "Building Your Leadership Brand," *Leader to Leader* (winter 2000), 40–46.

Weingand, Darlene E., and Noel Ryan. "Managerial Competences and Skills: A Joint Study in the United States and Canada," *Journal of Library Administration™* 6 (spring 1985): 23–44.

Wilder, Stanley. "The Age Demographics of Academic Librarians: A Profession Apart," *Journal of Library Administration™* 28, no. 3 (1999): 1–84.

Wilder, Stanley J. "New Hires in Research Libraries: Demographic Trends and Hiring Priorities," *ARL,* no. 221 [a bimonthly report on research library issues and actions from ARL, CNI, and SPARC, published by the Association of Research Libraries, Washington, D.C.] (April 2002): 5–8.

Williams, James F., II. "Leadership Evaluation and Assessment," *Journal of Library Administration™* 32, nos. 3 and 4 (2001): 145–67.

Winston, Mark D. "Recruitment Theory: Identification of Those Who Are Likely to Be Successful as Leaders," *Journal of Library Administration™* 32, nos. 3 and 4 (2001): 19–34.

Winston, Mark D., ed. "Leadership in the Library and Information Science Professions: Theory and Practice," *Journal of Library Administration™* 32, nos. 3 and 4 (2001): 1–186.

Winston, Mark D., and Lisa Dunkley. "Leadership Competencies for Academic Librarians: The Importance of Development and Fund-raising," *College & Research Libraries* 63 (March 2002): 171–82.

Winston, Mark D., and Teresa Y. Neely. "Leadership Development and Public Libraries," *Public Library Quarterly* 19, no. 3 (2001): 15–32.

BOOKS

Albritton, Rosie L., and Thomas W. Shaughnessy, eds. *Developing Leadership Skills: A Source Book for Librarians.* Englewood, Col.: Libraries Unlimited, 1990.

Association of College and Research Libraries. *1999 Academic Library Trends and Statistics for Carnegie Classification: Doctoral-Granting Institutions, Master's Colleges and Universities, Baccalaureate Colleges.* Compiled by Center for Survey Research [Thomas M. Guterbock, director; University of Virginia; Hugh A. Thompson, project coordinator]. Chicago: Association of College and Research Libraries, 2000.

Blank, Warren. *The 108 Skills of Natural Born Leaders.* New York: American Manage-
    ment Association, 2001.
Buros Institute of Mental Measurements. *Mental Measurements Yearbook.* 15 vols.
    Highland Park, N.J.: The Mental Measurements Yearbook, 1941–.
The Carnegie Foundation for the Advancement of Teaching. *The Carnegie Classifi-
    cation of Institutions of Higher Education.* Menlo Park, Calif.: Carnegie Foun-
    dation for the Advancement of Teaching, 2001.
Christian, Jeffrey E. *The Headhunter's Edge.* New York: Random House, 2002.
Corcodilos, Nick A. *Ask the Headhunter: Reinventing the Interview to Win the Job.*
    New York: Dutton, 1997.
Euster, Joanne R. *The Academic Library Director: Management Activities and Effec-
    tiveness.* New York: Greenwood Press, 1987.
Finlay, William, and James E. Coverdill. *Headhunters: Matchmaking in the Labor
    Market.* Ithaca, N.Y.: Cornell University Press, 2002.
Fulmer, Robert M., and Marshall Goldsmith. *Leadership Investment: How the World's
    Best Organizations Gain Strategic Advantage through Leadership Development.*
    New York: American Management Association, 2001.
Greenleaf, Robert K. *The Servant as Leader.* Indianapolis, Ind.: Robert Greenleaf
    Center, 1970.
Hackman, J. Richard. *Leading Teams: Setting the Stage for Great Performances.*
    Boston: Harvard Business School Press, 2002.
Hernon, Peter, and Robert E. Dugan. *An Action Plan for Outcomes Assessment in
    Your Library.* Chicago: American Library Association, 2002.
Hiatt, Peter, Ruth H. Hamilton, and Charlotte Wood. *Assessment Centers for Profes-
    sional Library Leadership: A Report to the Profession from the Career Develop-
    ment and Assessment Center for Librarians.* Chicago: American Library
    Association, 1993.
Hiebert, Murray, and Bruce Klatt. *Encyclopedia of Leadership: A Practical Guide to
    Popular Leadership Theories and Techniques.* New York: McGraw-Hill, 2001.
Klopp, Hap, and Tracy B. Klopp. *The Adventure of Leadership: An Unorthodox Busi-
    ness Guide by the Man Who Conquered "The North Face."* Stamford, Conn.:
    Longmeadow Press, 1991.
Kotter, John P. *John P. Kotter on What Leaders Really Do.* Boston: Harvard Business
    School Press, 1999.
Mech, Terrence F., and Gerard B. McCabe, eds. *Leadership and Academic Librarians.*
    Westport, Conn.: Greenwood Press, 1998.
Morrison, Perry D. *The Career of the Academic Librarian: A Study of the Social Ori-
    gins, Educational Attainments, Vocational Experience, and Personality Charac-
    teristics of a Group of American Academic Librarians.* Chicago: American
    Library Association, 1969.
Person, Ruth J., and Sharon J. Rodgers. *Recruiting the Academic Library Director.*
    Chicago: American Library Association, Association of College and Research
    Libraries, 1991.
Rothwell, William J., and H. C. Kazanas. *Building In-house Leadership and Manage-
    ment Development Programs: Their Creation, Management, and Continuous
    Improvement.* Westport, Conn.: Quorum, 1999.
Seidel, John. *The Ethnograph v5.0™: A User's Guide.* Thousand Oaks, Calif.: Scolari,
    1998.

Shea, Gordon F. *Mentoring: Helping Employees Reach Their Full Potential.* New York: American Management Association, AMA Membership Publications Division, 1994.

Sheldon, Brooke E. *Leaders in Libraries: Styles and Strategies for Success.* Chicago: American Library Association, 1991.

Stueart, Robert D., and Barbara B. Moran. *Library and Information Center Management.* Littleton, Col.: Libraries Unlimited, 1998.

Sydänmaanlakka, Pentti. *An Intelligent Organization: Integrating Performance, Competence and Knowledge Management.* Oxford: Capstone, 2002.

Training House, Inc. "Profile of Aptitude for Leadership." Training House, 1991.

Wachs, Esther. *Why the Best Man for the Job Is a Woman.* New York: HarperBusiness, 2000.

Wheatley, Margaret J. *Leadership and the New Science.* San Francisco: Berrett-Koehler, 1994.

Wilcox, John R., and Susan L. Ebbs. *The Leadership Compass: Values and Ethics in Higher Education.* ASHE-ERIC Higher Education Report no. 1. Washington, D.C.: George Washington University, School of Education and Human Development, 1992.

Yate, Martin. *Knock 'Em Dead 2003.* Avon, Mass.: Adams Media, 2002.

Zenger, John H., and Joseph Folkman. *The Extraordinary Leader: Turning Good Managers into Great Leaders.* New York: McGraw-Hill, 2002.

BOOK CHAPTERS

Hardesty, Larry. "The Future of Academic/Research Librarians: A Period of Transition—to What?" in *Global Issues in Twenty-First-Century Research Librarianship,* edited by Sigrún Klara Hannesdóttir. Helsinki, Finland: NORDINFO, 2002, 576–601.

ERIC DOCUMENTS

Wendel, Frederick C., Allan H. Schmidt, and James Loch. "Measurements of Personality and Leadership: Some Relationships." Lincoln, Nebr.: University of Nebraska, 1992 (ED 350 694).

PAMPHLETS AND DOCUMENTS

Association of Research Libraries, Office of Leadership and Management Services. *Changing Roles of Library Professions,* SPEC Kit 256. Washington, D.C.: Association of Research Libraries, 2000. Available: http://www.arl.org/spec/239/fly.html.

Association of Research Libraries. *Mentoring Programs in ARL Libraries,* SPEC Kit 239. Washington, D.C.: Association of Research Libraries, March 1999.

Frye Institute. *Leading the Information Revolution in Twenty-First Century Higher Education.* Atlanta, Ga.: Frye Institute, 2002.

Saulman, Sharon A., ed. *Sample Evaluations of Library Directors.* Chicago: American Library Association, American Library Trustee Association, 1997.

Soete, George J. *Evaluating Academic Library Directors*, SPEC Kit 229. Washington, D.C.: Association of Research Libraries, Office of Leadership and Management Services, May 1998.

Soete, George J. *Evaluating Library Directors: A Study of Current Practice and a Checklist of Recommendations*. OLMS Occasional Paper, no. 21. Washington, D.C.: Association of Research Libraries, Office of Leadership and Management Services, May 1998.

WEB RESOURCES

American Library Association, Association of College and Research Libraries, College Library Leadership Committee. Committee Minutes. Paper presented at annual meeting, Chicago: Association of College and Research Libraries, July 10, 2000. Available: http://www.austinc.edu/CLS/leadann00.html. Accessed 1 September 2002.

American Library Association, Association of College and Research Libraries/Harvard Leadership Institute of Harvard University's Graduate School of Education. "Highlights from Fourth Annual Institute." Chicago: Association of College and Research Libraries, February 2003. Available: http://www.gse. harvard.edu/~ppe/programs/acrl/program.html. Accessed 23 July 2003. Accessed 1 September 2002.

American Library Association, Association of College and Research Libraries, Personnel Administrators and Staff Development Officers Discussion Group, Ad Hoc Task Force on Recruitment and Retention Issues Group. "Recruitment, Retention and Restructuring: Human Resources in Academic Libraries." Paper presented in Chicago, 2002. Available: http://www.ala.org/acrl/ recruit-wp.html. Accessed 1 September 2002.

American Library Association. "The College Library Directors Mentor Program." Chicago: Association of College and Research Libraries, n.d. Available: http://www.lita.org/Content/NavigationM . . . ge_Library_Directors_ Mentor_Program.htm. Accessed 1 September 2002.

"APA News Release: What Makes a Good President?" Washington, D.C.: American Psychological Association, August 2000. Available: http://www.apa.org/ releases/presidents.html. Accessed 1 September 2002.

Association of Research Libraries, Office of Leadership and Management Services. Home page. Available: http://www.arl/org/olms/index.html; http://www. arl.org/training/index.html. Accessed 1 September 2002.

Association of Research Libraries, Office of Leadership and Management Services. NLM/AAHSL Leadership Fellows Program. Available: http://www. arl/org/olms/fellows/. Accessed 1 September 2002.

Assessment Systems Corporation. "Web-delivered Tests for Your Use When You Need Them!" n.p. Available: http://www.assess.com/panbypub.htm. Accessed 1 September 2002.

Association of Southeastern Research Libraries, Education Committee. "Shaping the Future: ASERL's Competencies for Research Libraries." Available: http:// www.aserl.org/statements/competencies/competencies.htm. Accessed 1 September 2002.

"Blake and Mouton Managerial Grid." Available: http://www.nwlink.com/
~donclark/leader/bm_model.html. Accessed 1 September 2002.

Buros Institute. "Tests." n.p. Available: http://www.unl.edu/buros/index18.html.
Accessed 1 September 2002.

Center for Creative Leadership. *Assessment Tools and Performance Support at a
Glance.* Greensboro, N.C.: Center for Creative Leadership, n.d. Available:
http://www.ccl.org/assessments. Accessed 1 September 2002.

CCI Assessment Group. "Leadership Assessment Survey." n.p. Available:
http://www.pantesting.com/products/CCI/las.asp. Accessed 1 September
2002.

Consulting Psychologists Press, Inc. Myers-Briggs Type Indicator®. n.p. Available:
http://www.cpp-db.com/products/mbti/index.asp. Accessed 1 September
2002.

Cromwell, Ron. "Librarian Shortage Looms," *The Enterprise.* Brockton, Mass.: n.p.,
n.d.. Available: http://enterprise.southofboston.com/archives (also see
http://www.bridgew.edu/NEWSEVNT?BSCNews1020215.htm). Accessed
1 September 2002.

Doffing, Heather. "Extended Hours Create Shortage of Librarians." *Daily Sundial
Online.* Available: http://sundial.csun.edu/sun/01s/051501ne4.htm.
Accessed 1 September 2002.

Gates, Kelly. "Librarians Are Finding Ample Opportunities," *Career Journal* (from
the *Wall Street Journal*). Available: http://www.careerjournal.com....
dustries/librarians/20001206-gates.html. Accessed 1 September 2002.

Human Synergistics/Center for Applied Research, Inc. *Leadership/Impact® (L/I).*
n.p. Available: http://www.hscar.com/li.htm. Accessed 1 September
2002.

InterLink Training and Coaching. "Leadership Assessment Tool." Anthem, Ariz.:
n.d. Available: http://www.interlinktc.com/assessment.html. Accessed 1 September 2002.

Jacobson, Jennifer. "A Shortage of Academic Librarians," *The Chronicle of Higher
Education: Career Network* (August 14, 2002): 1–4. Available: http://
chronicle.com/jobs/2002/08/200208/401c.htm. Accessed 1 September
2002.

Kaufman, Paula T. "Thoughts of Other Academic Library Directors," *Library Cultures Exploring Dimensions of Change: A Series of Lectures and Panels.* Ann
Arbor, Mich.: University of Michigan, School of Information, n.d.. Available:
http://www.si.umich.edu/library-cultures/academic/directors.html.
Accessed 1 September 2002.

Leadership That Works. "Training and Coaching for Success." n.p. Available:
http://www.leadershipthatworks.com/Coaching/C05CoachingAssessment.
htm. Accessed 1 September 2002.

"Leadership Self-Assessment." Alexandria, Va.: National School Boards Associations,
n.d. Available: http://www.nsba.org/sbot/toolkit/LeadSA.html. Accessed 1
September 2002.

McDowell, Melody M. "Help Wanted at Our Libraries," *Black Issues Book Review* 3
(March–April 2001): 78–79. Available: ProQuest (http://iibp.chadwyck.
com/fulltext?ACTION = byid&ID = 00033922. Accessed 1 September 2002.

NCS Assessments. "Clinical and Career Assessments: Campbell Interest and Skills Survey." n.p. Available: http://assessments.ncs.com/assessments/tests/ ciss.htm. Accessed 1 September 2002.

Neal, James G. "Turnover Trends: ARL Library Directors, 1948–2002." In *ARL Proceedings of the 141ˢᵗ Annual Meeting* [published by the Association of Research Libraries, Washington, D.C.] (October 2002). Available: http://www.arl.org/arl/proceedings/141/. Accessed 1 September 2002.

Northern Exposure to Leadership. Home page. Alberta, Calif.: Northern Exposure to Leadership. Available: http://www.ls.ualberta.ca/neli/instit.html. Accessed 1 September 2002.

Porrazzo, Jean. "Librarian Shortage Looms," *The Enterprise*. Brockton, Mass.: n.p., February 10, 2002. Available: http://enterprise.southofboston.com/ archives. Accessed 1 September 2002.

Pritchard, Sarah M. "Thoughts of Other Academic Library Directors," *Library Cultures Exploring Dimensions of Change: A Series of Lectures and Panels*. Ann Arbor, Mich.: University of Michigan, School of Information, n.d. Available: http://www.si.umich.edu/library-cultures/academic/directors.html. Accessed 1 September 2002.

R. E. Brown Company and Associates. Management/leadership survey. Available: http://www.rebrown.com/rebrown/orascale.htm. Accessed 1 September 2002.

Rodger, Joey. "Leadership, Libraries, and Literacy Programs: A Report of [a] Focus Group." Evanston, Ill.: Urban Libraries Council, 1999. Available: http://www.urbanlibraries.org/focus.PDF. Accessed 1 September 2002.

Rurak, Maura. "Demand Explodes for Librarians with High-tech Research Skills," *Career Journal* (from the *Wall Street Journal*). Available: http://www. careerjournal.com....dustries/librarians/19980825-rurak.html. Accessed 1 September 2002.

Team Management Services. "TMS Instruments." n.p. Available: http:// www.tms.co.nz/instruments.htm. Accessed 1 September 2002.

University at Buffalo, State University of New York, Leadership Development Center. "Resources—Tips and Tricks." n.p., July 24, 2001. Available: http://www.leadership.buffalo.edu/tips1.shtml. Accessed 1 September 2002.

University of Alabama at Birmingham, Presidential Search Advisory Committee. "Attributes of Leadership." n.p., n.d. Available: http://www.uasystem .ua.edu/Administrati...Search/attributes%20of%20leadership.htm. Accessed 1 September 2002.

Urban Libraries Council. "Executive Leadership Institute." Evanston, Ill.: Urban Libraries Council, 2002. Available: http://www.urbanlibraries.org/. Accessed 1 September 2002.

U.S. Department of Labor, Bureau of Labor Statistics. *Occupational Outlook Handbook 2002–03*. Washington, D.C.: GPO, 2002. Available: http:// stats.bls.gov/oco/ocos068.htm. Accessed 1 September 2002.

U.S. Office of Personnel Management. "360-Degree Program." Washington, D.C.: U.S. Office of Personnel Management, n.d. Available: http://www. leadership.opm.gov/content.cfm?cat = LAP. Accessed 1 September 2002.

Wilder, Stanley. "The Changing Profile of Research Library Professional Staff." *ARL*, nos. 208 and 209 [a bimonthly report on research library issues and actions from ARL, CNI, and SPARC, published by the Association of Research Libraries, Washington, D.C.] (February–April 2000). Available: http://www.arl.org/newsltr/208_209/chgprofile.html. Accessed 1 September 2002.

UNPUBLISHED MATERIAL

Anderson, A. J. Unpublished memorandum. Simmons College, Graduate School of Library and Information Science, Boston, 2002.

Frye, Billy E. "Some Reflections on Universities, Libraries, and Leadership." Paper presented at the University of Michigan, Ann Arbor, October 29, 1999.

MLA Leadership and Management Section Leadership Program. "Attributes of Library Leaders: Leadership Reconsidered: Developing a Strategic Agenda for Leadership in Health Sciences Libraries." Paper presented at Medical Library Association Conference, Dallas, Texas, May 22, 2002.

Matarazzo, James M. Unpublished paper. Simmons College, Graduate School of Library and Information Science, Boston, 2002.

INDEX

About the Authors

PETER HERNON is Professor, Simmons College Graduate School of Library and Information Science, Boston, where he teaches courses on research methods, U.S. government information, academic librarianship, and the evaluation of library services. He is the founding editor of *Government Information Quarterly*, the editor-in-chief of *The Journal of Academic Librarianship* (from 1994 through 2002), and the coeditor of *Library and Information Science Research*. He is the author of thirty-eight books and more than 170 articles.

RONALD R. POWELL is Professor, Library and Information Science Program, Wayne State University, where he teaches courses on academic libraries, research methods, and the evaluation of library resources and services. He is the author of a popular textbook, *Basic Research Methods for Librarians*, soon to be in its fourth edition. His research and publishing activities include education for academic research librarianship, measurement and evaluation, and research methods.

ARTHUR P. YOUNG is Dean of University Libraries, Northern Illinois University. He is the author of seven books and forty articles and book chapters. He has served as the editor of *ACRL Publications in Librarianship*, and he is the editor of *Beta Phi Mu Monographs*. His research interests include management, electronic resources, and library history. Dr. Young is the past president of the Illinois Library Association.